Bo

Here are tips on reading Bill Vincent's Books. Bill writes prophetically as God speaks. The grammar may be pushed but the message is spoken from the heart of God. Bill didn't want to lose the depth of revelation through extensive editing.

Glory: Expanding God's Presence: Discover How to Manifest God's Glory

Bill Vincent

Published by RWG Publishing, 2019.

While every precaution has been taken in the preparation of this book, the publisher assumes no responsibility for errors or omissions, or for damages resulting from the use of the information contained herein.

GLORY: EXPANDING GOD'S PRESENCE: DISCOVER HOW TO MANIFEST GOD'S GLORY

First edition. September 17, 2019.

Copyright © 2019 Bill Vincent.

Written by Bill Vincent.

Also by Bill Vincent

Building a Prototype Church: Divine Strategies Released
Experience God's Love: By Revival Waves of Glory School of the Supernatural
Glory: Expanding God's Presence
Glory: Increasing God's Presence
Glory: Kingdom Presence of God
Glory: Pursuing God's Presence
Glory: Revival Presence of God
Rapture Revelations: Jesus Is Coming
The Prototype Church: Heaven's Strategies for Today's Church
The Secret Place of God's Power
Transitioning Into a Prototype Church: New Church Arising
Spiritual Warfare Made Simple
Aligning With God's Promises
A Closer Relationship With God
Armed for Battle: Spiritual Warfare Battle Commands
Breakthrough of Spiritual Strongholds
Desperate for God's Presence: Understanding Supernatural Atmospheres
Destroying the Jezebel Spirit: How to Overcome the Spirit Before It Destroys You!
Discerning Your Call of God

Glory: Expanding God's Presence: Discover How to Manifest God's Glory

Glory: Kingdom Presence Of God: Secrets to Becoming Ambassadors of Christ

Satan's Open Doors: Access Denied

Spiritual Warfare: The Complete Collection

The War for Spiritual Battles: Identify Satan's Strategies

Understanding Heaven's Court System: Explosive Life Changing Secrets

A Godly Shaking: Don't Create Waves

Faith: A Connection of God's Power

Global Warning: Prophetic Details Revealed

Overcoming Obstacles

Spiritual Leadership: Kingdom Foundation Principles

Glory: Revival Presence of God: Discover How to Release Revival Glory

Increasing Your Prophetic Gift: Developing a Pure Prophetic Flow

Millions of Churches: Why Is the World Going to Hell?

The Supernatural Realm: Discover Heaven's Secrets

The Unsearchable Riches of Christ: Chosen to be Sons of God

Deep Hunger: God Will Change Your Appetite Toward Him

Defeating the Demonic Realm

Glory: Increasing God's Presence: Discover New Waves of God's Glory

Growing In the Prophetic: Developing a Prophetic Voice

Healing After Divorce: Grace, Mercy and Remarriage

Love is Waiting

Awakening of Miracles: Personal Testimonies of God's Healing Power

Deception and Consequences Revealed: You Shall Know the Truth and the Truth Shall Set You Free
Overcoming the Power of Lust
Are You a Follower of Christ: Discover True Salvation
Cover Up and Save Yourself: Revealing Sexy is Not Sexy
Heaven's Court System: Bringing Justice for All
The Angry Fighter's Story: Harness the Fire Within
The Wrestler: The Pursuit of a Dream
Beginning the Courts of Heaven: Understanding the Basics
Breaking Curses: Legal Rights in the Courts of Heaven
Writing and Publishing a Book: Secrets of a Christian Author
How to Write a Book: Step by Step Guide
The Anointing: Fresh Oil of God's Presence
Spiritual Leadership: Kingdom Foundation Principles Second Edition
The Courts of Heaven: How to Present Your Case
The Jezebel Spirit: Tactics of Jezebel's Control
Heaven's Angels: The Nature and Ranking of Angels
Don't Know What to Do?: Discover Promotion in the Wilderness
Word of the Lord: Prophetic Word for 2020
The Coronavirus Prophecy
Increase Your Anointing: Discover the Supernatural
Apostolic Breakthrough: Birthing God's Purposes
The Healing Power of God: Releasing the Power of the Holy Spirit
The Secret Place of God's Power: Revelations of God's Word
The Rapture: Details of the Second Coming of Christ
Increase of Revelation and Restoration: Reveal, Recover & Restore

Restoration of the Soul: The Presence of God Changes Everything

Building a Prototype Church: The Church is in a Season of Profound of Change

Keys to Receiving Your Miracle: Miracles Happen Today

The Resurrection Power of God: Great Exploits of God

Transitioning to the Prototype Church: The Church is in a Season of Profound of Transition

Waves of Revival: Expect the Unexpected

The Stronghold of Jezebel: A True Story of a Man's Journey

Glory: Pursuing God's Presence: Revealing Secrets

Like a Mighty Rushing Wind

Steps to Revival

Supernatural Power

The Goodness of God

The Secret to Spiritual Strength

The Glorious Church's Birth: Understanding God's Plan For Our Lives

God's Presence Has a Profound Impact On Us

Spiritual Battles of the Mind: When All Hell Breaks Loose, Heaven Sends Help

A Godly Shaking Coming to the Church: Churches are Being Rerouted

Relationship with God in a New Way

The Spirit of God's Anointing: Using the Holy Spirit's Power in You

The Magnificent Church: God's Power Is Being Manifested

Miracles Are Awakened: Today is a Day of Miracles

Prepared to Fight: The Battle of Deliverance

The Journey of a Faithful: Adhering to the teachings of Jesus Christ

Ascension to the Top of Spiritual Mountains: Putting an End to Pain Cycles

After Divorce Recovery: When I Think of Grace, I Think of Mercy and Remarriage

A Greater Sense of God's Presence: Learn How to Make God's Glory Visible

Do Not Allow the Enemy to Steal: To a Crown of Righteousness, a Crown of Thorns

There Are Countless Churches: What is the Cause of Global Doom?

Creating a Model Church: The Church is Undergoing Considerable Upheaval

Developing Your Prophetic Ability: Creating a Flow of Pure Prophetic Intent

Christ's Limitless Riches Are Unsearchable: God Has Chosen Us to Be His Sons

Faith is a Link Between God's Might and Ours

Increasing the Presence of God: The Revival of the End-Times Is Approaching

Getting a Prophecy for Yourself: Unlocking Your Prophecies with Prophetic Keys

Getting Rid of the Jezebel Spirit: Before the Spirit Destroys You, Here's How to Overcome It!

Getting to Know Heaven's Court System: Secrets That Will Change Your Life

God's Resurrected Presence: Revival Glory is Being Released

God's Presence In His Kingdom: Secrets to Becoming Christ's Ambassadors

God's Healing Ability: The Holy Spirit's Power is Being Released

God's Power of Resurrection: God's Great Exploits

Heaven's Supreme Court: Providing Equal Justice for All

Increasing God's Presence in Our Lives: God's Glory Has Reached New Heights

Jezebel's Stronghold: This is the Story of an Actual Man's Journey

Making the Shift to the Model Church: The Church Is In the Midst of a Major Shift

Overcoming Lust's Influence: The Way to Victory

Pursuing God's Presence: Disclosing Information

The Plan to Take Over America: Restoring, We the People and the Power of God

Revelation and Restoration Are Increasing: The Process That Reveals, Recovers, and Restores

Burn In the Presence of the Lord

Revival Tidal Waves: Be Prepared for the Unexpected

Taking down the Demonic Realm: Curses and Revelations of Demonic Spirits

The Apocalypse: Details about Christ's Second Coming

The Hidden Resource of God's Power

The Open Doors of Satan: Access is Restricted

The Secrets to Getting Your Miracle

The Truth About Deception and Its Consequences

The Universal World: Discover the Mysteries of Heaven

Warning to the World: Details of Prophecies Have Been Revealed

Wonders and Significance: God's Glory in New Waves

Word of the Lord

Why Is There No Lasting Revival: It's Time For the Next Move of God

A Double New Beginning: A Prophetic Word, the Best Is Yet to Come

Your Most Productive Season Ever: The Anointing to Get Things Done

Break Free From Prison: No More Bondage for the Saints

Breaking Strongholds: Taking Steps to Freedom

Carrying the Glory of God: Igniting the End Time Revival

Breakthrough Over the Enemies Attack on Resources: An Angel Called Breakthrough

Days of Breakthrough: Your Time is Now

Empowered For the Unprecedented: Extraordinary Days Ahead

The Ultimate Guide to Self-Publishing: How to Write, Publish, and Promote Your Book for Free

The Art of Writing: A Comprehensive Guide to Crafting Your Masterpiece

The Non-Fiction Writer's Guide: Mastering Engaging Narratives

Spiritual Leadership (Large Print Edition): Kingdom Foundation Principles

Desperate for God's Presence (Large Print Edition): Understanding Supernatural Atmospheres

From Writer to Marketer: How to Successfully Promote Your Self-Published Book

Unleashing Your Inner Author: A Step-by-Step Guide to Crafting Your Own Bestseller

Becoming a YouTube Sensation: A Guide to Success

The Art of Content Creation: Tips and Tricks for YouTube

Watch for more at
https://revivalwavesofgloryministries.com/.

Table of Contents

Title Page 1

Expanding Glory in the Earth 15

A Lifestyle of Glory 21

Being in the Presence of God 25

Distinguished by the Greater Glory 31

End Time Release of Signs and Wonders 35

Fiery Hot For God 47

How to Open the Windows of Heaven 57

There is a River 63

A Day of Open Doors 77

The Cloud is Touching Down 89

Revival Glory 93

Expanding Glory in the Earth

There is at all times a sound being released from earth to heaven as well as from heaven to earth – a divine exchange, so to speak.

In the unseen realm, it is in the form of energy patterns, waves, particles and though the vast majority of it is not heard with our natural ear, it is sensed by us because we are part of this existence.

What is coming from our end is "heard" by God and I believe that He has an ever flowing response back to us that we need to be aware of and "tune into" with our spirit man as to tap into that constant communion we can have with Him.

We often refer to it, as does Scripture, as "spirit to spirit, deep to deep". In John 17, Jesus prays concerning our oneness with Him, "...that they may be one just as We are one: I in them and You in Me."

Regardless of whether or not we are conscious of it, without that constant exchange this world as we know it would not even exist... "in Him all things consist." When God set up this whole existence of ours, He put it all in motion with the release of His sound, His Word, "Let there be Light."

In the beginning was the Word and the Word was with God and the Word was God. He was in the beginning with God. All things were made through Him and without Him nothing was made that was made. In Him was life and the life was the light of men. And the light shines in the darkness and the darkness did not comprehend [overcome] it. John 1:1-5.

Science is only just now catching up with the Word, but what they are discovering these days, especially in the quantum world of physics, is absolutely amazing as it pertains to scripture.

Even cell phones (the way sound travels), time travel and Jesus walking through walls and expanding of molecules are just the beginning of what God is about to do. God is going to connect these types of things and interlink them for a new level of Glory.

He released His sound, His Word out of Eternity and by all of this that we experience and all that has been experienced in all of history, along with what is to come is held together by it. Science calls it the zero energy point which is at the very center of the smallest particle. It is what keeps everything from collapsing all around us.

Jesus is the fleshly Manifestation of that Word – He IS the Word.

He is the image of the invisible God, the firstborn over all creation. For by Him all things were created that are in heaven and that are on earth, visible and invisible, whether thrones or dominions or principalities or powers. All things were created through Him and for Him. And He is before all things and in Him all things consist.

Colossians 1:15-17

It is all held together by Him, again, "...and in Him all things consist".

I had to look up that word "consist." I've heard this passage misquoted many times – I'VE misquoted this passage myself because of the way I've heard it said as often as "all things exist," rather than "consist." So I looked up the word consist because the Holy Spirit used that word specifically and the misquote drew my attention to it. The word consist means to be made up or composed, to be comprised or contained, to exist together or be capable of existing together. I found that very interesting – all of this is made capable of existing together only in Him.

I wanted to lay a scriptural foundation for some of what I wanted to say so that we don't get tripped up by some of the terminology I need to use to help unravel a bit of the mystery of this divine exchange of sound between heaven and earth.

This is in order to move into a focus on the coming sounds of worship being released to Heaven by way of intercession, hope, holy anticipation, faith, good works, etc., as well as the sounds of response from heaven to earth in the way of signs and wonders, manifestations (signs & wonders), angelic participation, revelation being released, etc. that are coming our way - the sounds of Heaven invading earth.

There is a sound of BREAKTHROUGH being released from Heaven in this hour that I believe can even be activated by our sounds of worship mixed with the sound of faith here on the earth.

Our agreement with Heaven's agenda will truly affect the outcome.

It may be strange to hear the phrase, "the sound of faith" or "the sound of good works," but energy that is released from these things really does have a sound. Worship is a sound, whether it is audible or inaudible to our natural ear, flowing from us to the Father. When we direct our hearts, our intent toward Him, even when we don't verbalize it, there are waves and/or vibrations that are released into the atmosphere that He sees, smells, hears, tastes – that He receives unto Himself.

Obviously, Scripture uses expression to describe the exchange between God and His creation – "Taste and see that the Lord is good." Our prayers are as an incense unto Him and He "fills His nostrils" with it. There are so many examples. But if you were to really look at what is happening at a level, that unseen realm, our words and sounds are releasing energy into the atmosphere that everything around us is affected by. I had gone through a period of time; I believe several months, where the Lord caused me to see and smell the spirit realm – particularly, the realm of emotions.

I actually saw the colors and smelled the fragrance that was released from people as they entertained emotions. If a person was angry I saw red coming from them with a foul scent accompanying it. Jealousy in a person released a greenish color, again with a particular foul smell. The most fowl scent of all came with self-pity. Demons would see and smell it and flock to the person to fuel the emotion. It worked as well on the flip side of that. Positive emotions released particular colors and pleasant fragrances, causing angels to come.

My point is that we see, hear and sense only in part what is taking place in the unseen realm. As I had all these experiences I was so confused. God revealed this revelation and then I thought, "I'm not going crazy after all and I am hearing God on all of this."

Something's up in the Spirit and it's a spirit to spirit understanding that He is giving us in this hour. Things have escalated drastically and there is a divine acceleration going on. I compare it to an earthquake.

If you were to say that the end of time as we know it is the center of the quake, then the closer we get to it the stronger and faster the ripples will be that pull us toward it. God is going to be releasing understanding at a greater pace. We are going to be much more accelerated to the unseen realm and I believe we will be more able to sense and discern what is happening there as a result of our actions and our words. We will see and hear more clearly His response and heaven's response, as we become more skilled in the ways of the spirit and the unseen realm.

I am setting the stage to move into some explanation of just how our words, our actions, our worship affect the unseen realm. The church is finally exploring that which was meant for us as believers from the beginning of time. We lost the understanding of His ways as we trusted more and more in the thoughts and ways of man....the opinions and traditional way of thinking in Greek-based philosophy.

We need to begin to pray and ask for the fullness of God to be released in our spirits that we might be enlightened to the way He meant for us to walk with Him even on this earth. He said He would have those who worship Him in spirit and in truth. There really is something on the horizon in the not so very distant distance. Worship will be key in releasing much of this. It will be used to change the atmosphere for the Light to penetrate the darkness "and the darkness will not comprehend [overcome] it." As He is lifted up He will draw all men unto Him. God is unlocking mysteries and allowing us to peer into things we've not understood until now. The nature of sound and how our words, our intent of heart, impacts the atmosphere.

The Lord set it all up in the very beginning with the release of the "let there be light" and we are just beginning to catch a glimpse of what that is. There is a line in a song that goes,

"Breaking the sound barrier, breaking the barrier of sound between heaven and the ground."

We've got to get in touch with the power of our words and yes, even the intent of our hearts.

As we align ourselves with the "sound of heaven" these things will begin to manifest on the earth.

A Lifestyle of Glory

There is a living and breathing generation that walks the earth today that is growing into its destiny as a Glory (presence based) Generation. They are a new wineskin that has been raised up for such a time as this. They are preaching the Gospel of the Kingdom, they are healing the sick, they are casting out unclean spirits, they are raising the dead and they are making disciples. They are fueled and compelled by the Love of Christ and the mighty Power of His Spirit. They are a generation extraordinaire that has learned the value of A Lifestyle of Glory.

The Glory of the Lord is a tangible reality available to every believer.

Another way to say this would be that the Presence of the Lord is real! It is a tangible reality on earth as it is in Heaven. Let's look at Exodus 33:10-14 which says that Moses prayed to the Lord,

Exodus 33:10-14 And all the people saw the cloudy pillar stand at the tabernacle door: and all the people rose up and worshipped, every man in his tent door. And the LORD spake unto Moses face to face, as a man speaketh unto his friend. And he turned again into the camp: but his servant Joshua, the son of Nun, a young man, departed not out of the tabernacle. And Moses said unto the LORD, See, thou sayest unto me, Bring up this people: and thou hast not let me know whom thou wilt send with me. Yet thou hast said, I know thee by name, and thou hast also found grace in my sight. Now therefore, I pray thee, if I have found grace in thy sight, shew me now thy way, that I may know thee, that I may find grace in thy sight: and consider that this nation is thy people. And he said, My presence shall go with thee, and I will give thee rest.

What a powerful passage of scripture demonstrating the tangible presence of the Lord that is not only available, but the heritage and destiny of every believer. Everyone saw, everyone heard, everyone experienced with their physical senses the Glory of the Lord. It was so beautiful and strong that everyone worshiped at the door of their tents. Entire families were witnessing the Glory of the Lord and worshiping in His Glorious Presence. We can't settle for anything less than this, the Glory of the Lord in all walks of life.

I looked up the word presence in vs. 14 and I was amazed at its meaning. It means the face of Yahweh that completely surrounds you. (In front of you, behind you, to the left and the right of you, above and beneath you.)

That blew me away when I read that Moses had asked for the Glory of Yahweh (or the face of Yahweh) to completely surround them as they journeyed into a land whose builder and maker was the Lord. He asked for the Glory of the Lord to be the mark that followed the nation of Israel.

In Matthew 28:20 Jesus says,

Teaching them to observe all things whatsoever I have commanded you: and, lo, I am with you alway, even unto the end of the world. Amen.

I looked up what that word "with" means in this verse and to my amazement it means after and/or behind. Virtually it means the same thing as stated in Exodus between Yahweh and Moses. And the great revelation in the New Covenant is that the former and latter rain has become one in Christ and now the Glory of Lord is a tangible reality around us and in us.

In this Lifestyle of Glory we see the Lord of Glory completely surrounding us and pouring out His Spirit upon everyone who asks, seeks and knocks. (Upon everyone who is hungry and thirsty.) Jesus' promise to everyone who asks is that they will receive. His promise to everyone who seeks is that they will find. His promise to everyone who knocks is that doors will be opened. He said blessed are the hungry & thirsty for they will be filled.

The very nature of this lifestyle stirs up hunger for seeking intimacy with Jesus. It produces a true desire for change and transformation.

A Lifestyle of Glory produces change that this world so desperately needs. Let's look at the change we see in the life of Peter after developing A Lifestyle of Glory. In Luke 5:8 we see Peter coming face to face with the Glory of the Lord in the person of Jesus and Peter falling down at Jesus' knees and saying, "depart from me Lord for I am a sinful man". In Luke 9:20 we see Peter declaring that Jesus is the Christ. In John 21:7 we see Peter jumping out of the boat and swimming to the resurrected Jesus who sat on the shore. In Acts 1:15 we see Peter standing up to preach among those who were gathered in the upper room. In Acts 2:14 we see Peter preaching and thousands were coming to the Lord. In Acts 3:6 we see Peter doing the works of Jesus and seeing the crippled man healed. In Acts 5:15 we see people who are being healed by lining up in the street and getting in Peter's shadow! That transformation is a result of developing A Lifestyle of Glory!

To develop this lifestyle you must learn to prioritize and place a daily demand on His Glory. Jesus said it best when He said the kingdom of heaven is like a pearl that when it is found is worth selling everything for. It is this Lifestyle of daily Glory that will spark the fires of Revival around the world and will awaken America to a third Great Awakening. It is this lifestyle that demonstrates the tangible presence of the Father to an unbelieving world. It is through this lifestyle that we will see a great grace released like never before and see entire cities come under the Greater Glory of the Lord. So today we place a demand on the Glory of the Lord and we consider it the greatest joy to let go of everything that we might live in.

Being in the Presence of God

If someone told you that you could experience increased intimacy with God by lying on your bed, relaxing and listening to worship music, what would you think? To some that suggestion might border on blasphemy. Do you equate pleasing God with working your fingers to the bone, serving on a bunch of committees, or having a disciplined quit time? If so, you probably feel guilty when you don't measure up to those self imposed standards, don't you? Many Christians are trapped in the Martha syndrome when they should be like Mary- sitting, resting at Jesus' feet and listening to his voice.

Through soaking, or the "contemplative life," we get more of God and His presence in our lives. I've found more power and revelation in quietness than in any other form of prayer. I believe the silent prayer of the heart is the highest form of prayer. Some Christians seldom enjoy this place of prayer because they never learn how to silence their hearts, minds and emotions and enter into true communion and fellowship with the Lord. I've heard from a great many prophets who say that when we learn to silence our thoughts, we have discovered the true secret to seeing in the spirit realm.

Through church history we can find a long trail of people who loved God's presence and passionately sought after Him. A group of these God Chasers were called the "Christian Contemplatives." They understood the biblical practice of meditation. Christians need to realize that the words meditate and meditations were in the book of Psalms long before the New Age movement existed. The Bible was the forerunner of meditation. Our ancient forefathers practiced meditation, as did the monks in the 1600s and 1700s.

If the word meditate makes you uncomfortable. Try substituting "to think about over and over and over again."

Who wants the power of God today? Who wants miracles, signs and wonders? Those who do, need to learn to be still. Now, think about this- the Bible talks about the Spirits of counsel and might. Might is the Power of God. God's might does not operate without his counsel. I am going to make an amazing statement: It isn't that the church doesn't have enough power; it's that the church doesn't wait to hear his counsel. We don't take time and wait in stillness to receive visions of what is going to happen in a service. The Spirit of counsel brings the Spirit of might. Waiting releases revelation, which ignites power. In the church today we are workers, not waiters. We are doers, not soakers. We are extremely busy people who can't silence our hearts and minds. It's time for God to bring us back to the art of being in His presence, He wants intimacy with us more than we want intimacy with him.

When I want to enter into the presence of God, I listen to music and lie on the floor on my back in total surrender. My focus is Jesus. I don't pray in tongues, nor do I make requests. I quiet my soul and wait patiently on the Lord. If we can't overcome the busyness of our minds, we'll never enter into the Spirit. It's the first thing we need to conquer.

Psalms 46:10 says, "Be still and know that I am God." The word still means "idle, quiet and alone," Here the word Know means "come to Know by experience or through intimate relationship." It also means "to perceive, to find or to see, to become known, or to be revealed." God had ordained more revelation. of him self in stillness than in any other form of prayer.

Think about the power of stillness. The most common hour of revelation in the Bible is 4:00 a.m. - the fourth watch. Jesus rose from the dead between 3:00 a.m. And 6:00 a.m.

God delivered the children of Israel from the hand of Egypt in the early hours and Jesus appeared near dawn to the disciples at sea. Often God comes when we're just dozing off or awakening – the quietest parts of the day. I came to understand God and the power of His anointing by lying in His presence in stillness and quietness. I not only received a greater revelation of who he is, but of who I am in Him.

In scripture the idea of being still before the Lord is also referred to as "waiting on the Lord." Waiting carries the idea of Hope and expectancy with it, it suggest lingering or remaining in one place, Knowing you are about to see or experience something. We are to wait with our thoughts on Jesus. Many of us who wait on God or "soak," play music in the background to help tune our hearts to him, though sometimes we wait in complete silence. Either way, our thoughts and emotions become quiet before the Lord and we focus all our attention on Jesus.

As you discover the incredible adventure of waiting on God, you will learn to rein in your mind when it begins to wonder. But press in, because after about two or three weeks of setting aside one to three hours a day of contemplation and mediation, you will begin to master your mind. It's a discipline and it takes time to cultivate this lifestyle of waiting. When you learn to overcome distractions to focus on Jesus, you will have a breakthrough in the spirit unlike at any other time in your life.

Hebrews 12:2 describes contemplation in another way: "looking unto Jesus, the author and finisher of our faith." Yes, the soaking meditation I described involves looking unto Jesus and gazing at him. To gaze suggest turning your eyes away from other things and fixing them on something and staring at it. The word gaze carries the idea of studying intently - "seeing with the eyes and with the mind, perceiving, knowing and becoming acquainted by multiple experiences."

Jesus is the author of our faith, but how does he become the finisher of our faith? I believe we need to have multiple experiences in the revelatory realm. For that to occur, we have to remain in his presence- wait in quietness and stillness. Isaiah 64:4 says that God is a God who acts for the one who waits for him.

In my experience as I soaked and waited on God, He began to act- things got done and prayers were answered. To be honest, for a while I thought, All I am doing is lying around in the presence. I'm not doing anything. I'm not praying in tongues or reading the Bible. But that was exactly what I needed. Isn't it interesting that the thing that gets God to move is waiting? I get more out of waiting in stillness and quietness than I do out of three hours of prayer.

Some people don't feel that they truly connect with God unless they are doing something like interceding, praying in tongues, worshiping, or reading the Bible.

The minute they stop, they feel that prayer is over and God is gone; they don't know how to stay in the presence. When I say, "Let's be quiet in his presence for half an hour," they start speaking in tongues. They are programmed to do something! The Bible says, "but those who wait on the Lord shall renew their strength, they shall mount up with wings like eagles, they shall run and not be weary. They shall walk and not faint" (Isaiah 40:31) It all happens while we're waiting. Here is another verse for you: "In returning and rest you shall be saved: in quietness and confidence shall be your strength" (Isaiah 30:15). If you want to enter into the Supernatural realm, Practice soaking and meditating for an hour a day- add that to what you already do.

Distinguished by the Greater Glory

Are you desperate, or even hope for the raw authentic power of God? The Father longs for a generation to arise who live only to see His Kingdom come on earth as it is in heaven. The Father longs for YOU to arise and hear His invitation to come into the glory today, yet not just any glory–His Greater Glory! In this teaching you will learn about the greater glory, which is available to you, and keys to unlock it in your life!

There have been many authentic moves of God throughout history. One that comes to mind is the Cane Ridge Revival of 1800. The power of God moved so mightily among some Presbyterian ministers during a sacramental meeting that services were extended for weeks. Many people from all denominations flooded the area so much that at times there were over 25,000 people attending the meeting! Thousand of people came to Jesus and hundreds laid slain in the Spirit. It was said that so many people laid on the ground before the Lord all at once that it looked like men slain on a battle field! It was also said that at times when thousands were in unity in worship all would break out into loud cries, shouts and praises to the Lord and could literally be heard for miles around! That's what I call "Authorized Fire".

In Leviticus 9:23-10:1, we read some dynamic verses and can learn multiple principles about the fire of God. In fact, we can read where the authentic authorized fire of God comes from and where it doesn't. Let's take a look.

(v.23) Moses and Aaron then went into the Tent of Meeting. When they came out, they blessed the people; and the glory of the Lord appeared to all the people. (v.24) Fire came out from the presence of the Lord and consumed the burnt offering and the fat portions on the altar. And when all the people saw it, they shouted for joy and fell facedown. (10:1) Aaron's sons Nadab and Abihu took their censers, put fire in them and added incense; and they offered unauthorized fire before the Lord.

In this story there are two types of fire. The first, which came from the presence of the Lord, it consumed the burnt offerings and fat portions on the altar. Also, it caused unspeakable joy and praise among the people in such a great way that they all fell facedown–this was a good service or session. If it were in modern times it would have been an exhilarating worship service where the presence of God would have be so thick and heavy, that the preacher could only say a few words then lay down on the platform while people worshipped the Lord through their praises, shouts, dancing, tears and laying facedown. I love it when this happens.

This is the fire that only comes out of one place, (v.24) Fire came out from the presence of the Lord... .

The second, was a fire that was put in censers by Aaron's sons Nadab and Abihu. But notice it did not come from the presence of the Lord; rather, it was a man made, self produced fire. It could of looked, smelled, moved and made the same noise as the fire they just witnessed that came out of the presence and glory of the Lord, yet it wasn't. What they offered was an unauthorized fire and they were terminated because of this act. I can only imagine what they were thinking, but maybe they saw their father Aaron being used as an instrument with Moses to release a blessing on the people. From this, the glory of the Lord appeared in such a strong way that the fire of God was evoked on the earth and many people shouted for joy and they thought to themselves, "There are two of them and there is two of us; we need this power, lets get some fire".

You see, there is reserved revival fire in heaven that God wants to pour out on the earth and on His people, to cause such an awe and ultimate Kingdom culture in every sphere of society like the fire that Moses and Aaron were a part of. It is authorized fire and this is the only fire and glory that is going to change your life, situation and cause such a miraculous release to everyone around you! This is the fire and glory that transformed millions and change me into a raw radical lover of Jesus and son of God. This is the fire of God that comes out of His presence and glory and it is only reserved for those that will say, "I want the authentic raw power of God; I want the greater glory!"

But the only place this unique holy fire comes from is the presence of His Glory. Moses and Aaron literally just came out of the secret place, the Tent of Meeting. They were personally experiencing the presence of Yahweh and it was from this realm they blessed the people. We can only wholeheartedly bless or minister to people by first being in the Tent of Meeting–the secret place.

It is out of this realm the blessing is extended for Moses and Aaron and this same goes for us. Moses and Aaron blessed them and from the blessing came the glory of God. Blessing, honor, love and unity is a key of the release of a private secret place glory into a public quarter amongst people, where it becomes a corporate glory. These are some great keys to an outpouring and the glory of God, but I want to focus this point on that there is an authentic fire that comes from the presence. This fire is a part of the greater glory reserved for those who will say, "Lord, show us your Glory" and "Lord, distinguish us by your presence"; who will not settle for unauthorized fire like Aaron's sons Nadab and Abihu.

I believe God is raising up an end-time vast mighty army to carry this greater glory into the entire earth! You are called to a greater fire, greater presence and greater glory!

I believe this and find it interesting that Moses asked the Lord to go with him and to distinguish His people from all other people on the earth by His presence.

(v.15) "If your presence does not go with us, do not send us up from here. (v.16) How will anyone know that you are pleased with me and with your people unless you go with us? What else will distinguish me and your people from all the other people on the face of the earth?"-Exodus 33:15, 16

End Time Release of Signs and Wonders

Only believe..." (Luke 8:50). That's the door that opens up the spiritual realm, which brings all the miracles and all the signs and all the wonders. God wants us to believe like the saints of old and He wants to release miracles like we see from the beginning to the end of the Bible. After all, this is the inheritance of His sons and daughters! Therefore, God wants to challenge our belief system and our level of faith because He wants to make the supernatural natural as common place.

We are living in an exciting time! It's the last days- the only days that each of us has to serve the Lord. And what happens in the last days? God pours out His Spirit on all flesh!

Acts 2:17-21 And it shall come to pass in the last days, saith God, I will pour out of my Spirit upon all flesh: and your sons and your daughters shall prophesy, and your young men shall see visions, and your old men shall dream dreams: And on my servants and on my handmaidens I will pour out in those days of my Spirit; and they shall prophesy: And I will shew wonders in heaven above, and signs in the earth beneath; blood, and fire, and vapour of smoke: The sun shall be turned into darkness, and the moon into blood, before that great and notable day of the Lord come: And it shall come to pass, that whosoever shall call on the name of the Lord shall be saved.

"Whoever calls upon the name of the Lord shall be saved." Does this refer to a day yet to come or a day that is here? I believe we are living in the outpouring of God's Spirit right now. He is releasing prophecy, visions and dreams to his people today: "I will pour out My Spirit on all flesh." Sons and daughters are prophesying, young men are having visions and old me are dreaming dreams.

God's ultimate purpose is that we all will prophesy and have dreams and visions. What we are seeing now is progressive; it's a process. I believe that this divine promise is available today for anyone who is ready to receive it. A day is coming for the church when all flesh will come into the dimensions of visions, dreams, healings and miracles. This calling goes way beyond the dimension of commonplace prophetic words, the still small voice, impressions, words of knowledge, prophetic exhortation, or even "thus says the Lord" prophecies spoken in the first person (as if God was speaking the words.)

For instance, today, every believer should be having profound, detailed, accurate words of knowledge for their server in the restaurant. Every believer should be having visions and dreams. Every Christian should be participating in healings and miracles. These experiences are available to all of us now.

All of us have an opportunity to participate in the release of this prophetic dimension which will come with signs and wonders. We are destined to carry that supernatural anointing, to walk in the reality of the spirit of wisdom and revelation and to have the eyes of our heart opened to see into the heavens. This is our inheritance. According to Scripture, God endorses ministry through signs and wonders:

Acts 2:22 Ye men of Israel, hear these words; Jesus of Nazareth, a man approved of God among you by miracles and wonders and signs, which God did by him in the midst of you, as ye yourselves also know:

This scripture speaks of the days when God confirmed and endorses Jesus' ministry with miracles, signs and wonders. According to John 17, we are just as loved by the Father as Jesus is; we are just as much a child and just as much a joint-heir. Jesus asked this of the Father:

John 17:23 I in them, and thou in me, that they may be made perfect in one; and that the world may know that thou hast sent me, and hast loved them, as thou hast loved me.

The Father wants to endorse ministry in North America with miracles, signs and wonders – He wants us to reach for this inheritance. We need to say, "Thank You Lord that it's mine." The supernatural needs to become a part of our consciousness, part of our everyday thinking. We need to think about open heavens, angels, visions and dreams. We need to talk about miracles, power and healings. We need to thank God for angels and for the prophetic.

Yes, we are living in an exciting time! God wants to anoint you for prophetic vision and to give you spiritual eyes.

As the Lord opens the eyes of your heart, you will come into the reality of the spiritual realm. God wants to make you naturally supernatural. It's time for you to launch into new realms of the spirit.

Did you know your destiny is to be a sign and a wonder? We were created to see them and we were created to be them. So let's delve deeper into this passage:

Isaiah 8:18 Behold, I and the children whom the LORD hath given me are for signs and for wonders in Israel from the LORD of hosts, which dwelleth in mount Zion.

Now look what happens if we are not for signs and wonders:

Isaiah 8:19 And when they shall say unto you, Seek unto them that have familiar spirits, and unto wizards that peep, and that mutter: should not a people seek unto their God? For the living to the dead?

Listen! When we're not for signs and wonders people go to wizards, mediums and dead gods. They consult the dead on behalf of the living, rather than consulting the living God.

So we need to live out our spiritual inheritance and be signs and wonders; then the world will turn to the church for revelation.

We need to understand the reality of the supernatural, open heavens and the heavenly glory. We should be reaching for the place in the spirit where supernatural signs and wonders take place. That is the anointing that God wants to release. Are you ready for that?

The apostle Paul was ready! He said that he had fully preached the gospel because his preaching was accompanied with signs and wonders by the power of God (Romans 15:17-29). We need to chew on that for a while because if we haven't preached the gospel with signs and wonders then we actually haven't fully preached the gospel.

In the context of the gospel presentation, we should always see the manifestation of God's power.

Matthew 9:35 And Jesus went about all the cities and villages, teaching in their synagogues, and preaching the gospel of the kingdom, and healing every sickness and every disease among the people.

Notice that Jesus preached the gospel and healed every sickness and disease. In every reference where Jesus proclaimed the gospel, we see the demonstration of the kingdom. In my ministry I teach my disciples, "Power first then the Words. Go in and prophesy first, or demonstrate the power of God first in some way." In the church, there's been such a lack of the demonstration of God's power. Our preaching often isn't effective in the church today because so many people's attitude is "been there, done that, bought the t-shirt." Their minds and hearts are often already closed five minutes into the service.

The church needs to see a demonstration of God's power and so does the world outside of the church!

And so God, in His great mercy, backs up the salvation message with signs, wonders and various miracles (Acts: 2:22, 5:12, 14:3; Hebrews 2:4). That is the gospel message.

As I've said, Jesus didn't just preach the gospel to the poor and stop at that (Matthew 4:23, 9:35); He set an example of what we should do. We are the generation that should enter into "greater works than these" (John 14:12). In the church today, we have limited the gospel to only preaching, but it shouldn't be isolated from these other kingdom manifestations. According to Jesus and Paul, preaching, healing and miracles are a package deal.

Therefore, if you want to know if the kingdom has come to your life or your church, just ask this question. "Do the lame walk; do the blind see; are AIDS suffers healed; are the dead raised; and do the poor hear the gospel?" Look for the signs and wonders of the manifestation of His kingdom.

God is about to reap a great end-time harvest.

Revelations 14:15 And another angel came out of the temple, crying with a loud voice to him that sat on the cloud, Thrust in thy sickle, and reap: for the time is come for thee to reap; for the harvest of the earth is ripe.

I believe that healings and miracles are the sickle which God is going to use to reap the end-time harvest. The world is hungry for the supernatural realm. Unfortunately, to the world, the church has no power. That's why all the psychic hotlines are busy and the New Age movement is growing dramatically. However, although it looks as though the church is weak in comparison to the works of darkness, this is a false impression!

God spoke to me from scripture that by His great power He is going to eat up the devil's counterfeit signs and wonders just like Aaron's rod did when it turned into a serpent and ate up the sorcerer's rod (Exodus 7:8-12).

The world today is looking to false religions, cult leaders and ungodly doctrines. But the true God is going to send His "serpent" into the world to eat up the counterfeit. There will be such an outpouring of God's healing power and prophetic words that the false will be eaten up by the true signs and wonders of a victorious church. The world will know that healing for their body is in the church. In some places, hospitals and clinics will close. The spirit of truth will be seen overcoming the spirit of error (1 John 4:6) and the world will finally know what is true and false.

I see leaders of occult movements turning to the truth of Jesus Christ because of the signs and wonders taking place in the church. They will see, like Simon the sorcerer saw, that we flow in real power (Acts 8: 17-19).

This outpouring of power will be so great that the Baals of today will be shown up by the genuine miracles of the church like Elijah on Mt. Carmel. Let's remember that the power of God came because the fervent prayer of a righteous man avails much (James 5:16). Let's pray fervently that this same great anointing of boldness and power would rest upon God's people today.

Signs-prophets are those who carry two dimensions: first, their whole life becomes a sign and they live out the message that God has called them to illustrate God's relationship to His unfaithful people (Hosea 1:2). Second, these prophets carry with them the reality of miracles, signs and wonders. If you watch the news when people come to town, quite often you'll see a change in the weather patterns – freak storms, floods, tremors, plagues, or other signs and wonders.

Today, signs-prophets are again beginning to partner with God in fulfilling this verse:

Acts 2:19 And I will shew wonders in heaven above, and signs in the earth beneath; blood, and fire, and vapour of smoke:

I believe that God is releasing this signs-and-wonders dimension in the earth today to validate the visions and dreams of the prophets. He is increasing the authority of true prophetic words in the midst of all the prophetic fluff and He is granting signs through true healing ministries.

As well, God is granting signs through weather patterns and earthquakes.

Sometimes the Lord calls us to roar just as He does (Joel 3:16; Hosea 11:10). At God's leading, we can release a roar by fait just as we would a victory shout (Joshua 6:5). A roar like this often releases a holy indignation within our spirits, as a declaration to the enemy that "enough is enough!" Roaring only looses promises that have been tied up, but it also tears down demonic principalities.

When we roar like a lion, something happens in the spirit realm. Jesus is the Lion of the Tribe of Judah and sometimes He causes His Spirit to rise up in our hearts with a groan or a roar of judgment on principalities.

We must realize that God does not cause natural disasters. However, when God wants to bring change or to release revival, there will always be spiritual war in the heavens as demonic principalities in the second heaven resist God's advancing plans. When there's war, there are causalities. We don't always understand why people get hurt. When Jesus cast the demon out of a child in Luke 9:42 (NAS), "the devil threw him down and tare him." In the same way, when God deals with demonic forces in the heavens, a tearing takes place in the spiritual realm which sometimes manifests in destructive ways on earth. The enemy desires to bring destruction and to prevent God's plan for revival. However, in spite of the battle, God's plans will always come to pass.

God is sending signs of revival in Christian meetings in the form of gold dust, diamonds, feathers and the people are growing in the passion for the Lord as well as faith for the wave of revival that is coming.

What does all of this mean? We need to understand that God's judgments are released as answers to prayer to ultimately bring blessing and to fulfill His promise. God reveals future events-secrets- to His friends and to His prophets (Amos 3:7). As a result of repentance and travailing prayer by God's people, the Lord will judge demonic principalities over areas. Often those supernatural judgments are manifested in the natural through disasters.

The Lord is making His name known against His adversaries and releasing blessings on His people in those areas. He wants us to have an idea about what He's doing, so He gives us signs on earth of what He is doing in the spiritual realm.

These prophets may walk in a greater dimension of power than most believers, but we are all called to start living in the supernatural realm in these end days. All of God's children were created for signs and wonders, not just the signs-prophets.

We are to be a sign, a living epistle and a prophetic picture in the earth. We are to be a manifestation of the supernatural realm spilling over and breaking into the natural realm everywhere we go-the marketplace, work, business, school, the mall, or the hospital. We should be carrying signs and wonders because we carry the reality of the kingdom of heaven within us (Luke 17:21). Though I am on the earth, in my mind I am in heaven. I am operating in that realm in the anointing of the spirit of wisdom and revelation.

God wants to give us the anointing of the supernatural! As I said earlier, God is granting signs through true healing ministries.

Take for instance, the "Voice of Healing" revival in America that took off in the 50's and 60's with Oral Roberts, Jack Coe, A.A. Allen, R.T. Ritchie and Gordon Lindsay. Tens of thousands of people packed into tents all across America.

William Branham was a forerunner of signs and wonders ministry seen in that day. In 1946, an angel visited this poor uneducated, stuttering man and imparted a healing anointing.

But it wasn't just a healing anointing-they called William Branham a prophet of notable signs and wonders. He moved in more accurate realms of revelation than almost any one else of his time. Some say his gifting was one hundred percent accurate.

In his meetings, the people would line up and Branham would begin to go into visions and tell them many details of their lives. He spoke out "words of knowledge" only a sign that the Lord would hear them. Often Branham wouldn't even pray for their people; yet they would walk out of the meetings healed.

The miracles, signs and wonders in Branham's ministry, released through visions, validated Branham's ministry as people received dramatic healing signs in their bodies. I believe that the Holy Spirit is beginning to release this same supernatural dimension through believers today.

Through this experience, I believe the Lord is saying He's going to validate the prophetic words, visions and dreams of the prophets by releasing signs and wonders on the earth beneath. It's going to become commonplace for the church today.

As you've been reading this book, I really believe the Lord has been preparing you for encounters with a whole new anointing for revelation and for the Spirit of the Lord to rest on your life afresh. The Holy Spirit wants to give you a continual sense of what the Father is doing. He wants to pull back the curtain and let you see into the Heavens.

The Lord showed me that His secrets and His power are for those who have sweet, satisfying companionship with Him. "The secret of the Lord is with those who fear Him and He will show them His covenant" (Psalms 25:14). He's only going to trust His friends with the signs and wonders ministry: "No longer do I call you servants, for a servant does not know what his master is doing; but I have called you friends, for all things that I heard from My Father I have made known to you" (John 15:5).

God came down and visited Moses. He would speak to Moses as a friend and speaks to a friend, face-to-face. I believe that today, God is calling His people into an intimate friendship with Him, in which He can begin to speak to them in trust, face-to-face. "Those who are My real friends, I trust and I give them understanding of what I'm doing in the earth today," He has said to me. "I'm going to trust My friends with end-time power in the earth. It's going to be based on intimacy and friendship."

Signs, wonders and prophetic insights are all going to be in the realm of friendship. Although the visitation in my hotel room was a profound supernatural encounter, the Father's greatest message to me was that He wanted to be my intimate friend.

I believe that as we all enter this place of friendship with Him, the Father will also release us into the fullness of our destiny. That destiny includes not only sharing the gospel, but also, as part of the gospel package, performing signs and wonders. And there's more- we don't just do signs and wonders; we are to be a sign and a wonder! God wants us to have and to be the "genuine article" so the world can know there's revelation and understanding in the church.

With the end-time release of signs and wonders happening, we won't even need to preach the gospel because it will be apparent to the unbelievers that there is a living God in heaven intervening in the affairs of mankind!

Fiery Hot For God

Deep, raw, hunger for intimacy with God is only satisfied through expression. However, many find it difficult to express this desire or any other things of the heart. The psalmists did this very well and I believe this is why the psalms are so popular. They not only provide us with models to follow, but they also inspire us to voice out our own deepest feelings and aspirations. Psalms express heart cries, wonderings, longings, thanksgiving, praise and satisfy the innermost yearnings to do what we were created for, worship the king. They take us from the heights to the depths and we can feel God Himself cry with us. It's as if the psalms give us a "kick start" because they help our emotions come to the surface as we identify with the cry of the Psalmists.

With this in mind, let's examine two particular verses that were composed with great sensitivity by a priestly family, the sons of Korah. The first verse found in Psalms 42: "As the deer pants for the water brooks, so pants my soul for You, O God. My soul thirsts for God, the living God" (Psalms 42:1, 2). The word pant means more than just breathing rapidly and heavily. It also means to yearn eagerly. Do you yearn eagerly for God? Are you thirsty for the living God? The second verse found in Psalms 84:2 also describes an intense longing for God's presence. "My soul longs, yes, even faints for the courts of the LORD; my heart and my flesh cry out for the living God."

Listen. It's time to know Him and be known by Him! God is issuing a personal invitation to you (Revelations 3:20). God is looking for a response. He is welcoming you to come into His presence to spend time with Him, alone, so that your love and passion for Him will reach new heights. If you are willing to say, "Yes," He will fan the flames of desire for intimacy with Him.

The Holy Spirit revealed to me that when we really desire His presence, He will cause awesome things to happen and will release even those things we're not expecting. Isaiah the prophet said: "Oh, that You would rend the heavens! That You would come down! That the mountains might shake at Your presence" (Isaiah 64:1). Yes! "Oh God, tear open the heavens and come down!" Isn't that what we all want?

The heavens opened over my own life in 2008 and God indeed caused great things to happen, things I hadn't expected, as well as things I'd asked for. Today, I carry my open heaven with me; I live and minister under an open heaven and God continues to surprise me day-to-day. I believe God's favor came upon me because I pursued His presence and nothing more. I desired Him alone, above all else. I sought His presence, not the blessings His presence brought. Today, people often pursue God for increased benefits and sometimes that's their motivation for their time in the secret place. However, that's not a hunger for God, that's a hunger for the fruit. Yes, there are many blessings in that place, but we'll only see the face of God and receive His kiss of love when we desire Him alone.

Perhaps God is revealing that your love relationship with Him is alive, spontaneous and passionate. That's great! You might even be thinking how can I take that fire that I already have in my heart and make it an inferno? On the other hand, God may be revealing that your level of desire and passion for Him is weakening. If so, God wants to arouse and awaken your love for Him. He wants your passion to strengthen.

"When I passed by you again and looked upon you, indeed your time was the time of love; so I spread My wing over you and covered your nakedness. Yes, I swore an oath to you and entered into a covenant with you and you became Mine" (Ezekiel 16:8). Although this message from God was spoken to the inhabitants of Jerusalem through Ezekiel (the prophet), it's still a significant "now word" for us today. It reveals so well God's heart of compassion and love toward us.

God wants you to know that He sees your vulnerability and He is covering you with His love and protection. That's the bottom line. You are loved! You are covered! And His love for you is whole-hearted. By that, I mean His love isn't just talk. He doesn't just whisper empty words into our ear! God is good! He backs up His words with actions, confirmations and evidences of His love that we can see or perceive.

He wants the same from us- He doesn't want us to love on Him with just a lot of talk and no action, or no passion and emotion either. God wants us fervent in spirit. He wants us to be fiery hot! The word fervent means it's like an erupting, boiling volcano! Are you an erupting, burning volcano-fiery hot? Boiling over is the word!

The Father has created a holy and intimate place in the spirit that the world cannot penetrate. It's called the secret place of His presence. It's reserved for us, true believers in Jesus Christ and it's a place of freedom where our love for Jesus can intensify our intimacy and cause overflowing life-giving joy!

I'm continually in this place of intimacy and my cry is "God, make me fiery joy! I want to be like John the Baptist. I was to be a burning, shining lamp" (John 5:35) Listen. God not only wants to brand many believers with His fiery touch,

He also wants to impact lives deeper than we ever thought possible. He wants to fan the flame in your heart!

So it's time to ask God for new passion, new fire and the gift of holy hunger.

In my life, this holy hunger caused such a passion in my heart for the one thing that is far above anything else and that is God's precious presence. Like David, my deepest cry to God is: "My God, please take not thy Holy Spirit from me" (Psalms 51:11) I've wept as I've prayed this prayer hundreds of times. "God please, I've received such an outpouring of Your grace; if that were gone, if Your Spirit lifted from my life, it would all be over. Please take not thy Holy Spirit from me." And He hasn't.

We can choose to stir up our love for God! To stir up our love means to raise up, to excite, to rouse, arouse to action, we become as a musical instrument warmed up to play. Did you know that the love and passion that you have in your heart for Him needs to be warmed up? The question is: How do you warm up your love or arouse your heart for Him even more?

In Song of Songs, Solomon writes: "do not stir up nor awaken love until it pleases" (Song. Of Songs 3:5b) It's as if he is saying, "Don't let love come alive in your heart until you are ready for it. It's going to cost you. Love will cost you; so don't awaken love until you are ready. If you are not ready to abandon yourself to Him then don't awaken it."

How many of you are ready to be lovers of God? You see, it's our choice whether we're going to love God. It's our choice whether we're going to be passionate and hungry. We must choose whether we're going to let our love be aroused for God or not. Bottom line-we choose.

GLORY: EXPANDING GOD'S PRESENCE: DISCOVER HOW TO MANIFEST GOD'S GLORY

To steward means to responsibly give away or share the blessings of God. With God's Spirit resting upon my life, I've learned how to steward the flame in my heart. By that I mean, I cherish His presence in my life and I want everyone else to experience God's presence, too. This is my prayer for you!

When we choose to have our passion stirred up, there's going to be the expectation that if God imparts a holy hunger into out heart, we're going to have to steward it. The question is this: Do you know how to be a steward of love? Do you know how to be a steward of passion? Do you know how to be a steward of the desire and the hunger that you have in your heart for Him? It's going to take time, passion, sacrifice and commitment.

God doesn't want dull lovers or insensitive stewards of His blessings. He wants us fiery hot! But so much of the church today is lukewarm (Revelations 3:15, 16). Many know very well that they aren't hungry or desperate enough for God's presence in their lives. Yet, they barely realize that it is only by the grace of God His love can come upon their hearts and supernaturally empower them to love the way that He wants them to. So how do we awaken and stir up love? Listen, we can't love passionately unless we're intoxicated with the influence of His affection.

My prayer for you is that you would receive a "holy hunger" for intimacy with God. I believe God is going to pour out this gift according to your measure of hunger, according to your desperation.

Holy hunger goes hand-in-hand with God's desire to help you stir up and awaken your passion for Him. God deserves our love more than anything in this world. He is worthy.

Listen, at this very moment, Jesus Christ is preparing a place for us in our Father's house. We're going to be with Him forever (John 14:2, 3). Therefore, it's time to make ourselves ready, even as a bride would get ready for her wedding day and her husband-to-be.

The story of the Shulammite bride in the Songs of Solomon is filled with imagery and intimacy. The confidence of the bride and the spouse in each other gives us a valuable insight into how to fan the flames of desire and stir and awaken our love for God.

1. Get started: "My beloved spoke and said to me, 'Rise up my love, my fair one and come way'" (Song of Songs 2:10). God is the initiator. He speaks to us. Having said that, though, we still need to get started by responding to Him. So in that sense, it starts with you. How hungry are you? Set a time to meet with God. Set a place. Rise up! Purpose this in your heart and say, "God you are my God! Early will I seek You!" Don't wait for the grace to pray. Pray for the grace to pray. Rise up and say, "I will stir myself up to take hold of God." There are times when the presence of God comes and it's like four hours of glorious Holy Ghost! Then there are other times when you need to purpose in your heart to rise up and pray four hours because you're hungry. So sometimes it just starts with you. Be disciplined.

2. Remember God's Love for You: "We will remember your love" (Song of Songs 1:4). Something happens in our heart when we remember visitations when we remember the promises of God. We are stirred when we think back to those days in which we really were experiencing the "rapture of love."

Remembering God's love for us is so important, because in the remembering, our hearts are touched once again with God's faithfulness towards us. This helps us to trust Him and to stir up and awaken lost love.

3. Be A Steward of His Presence: We need to allow the presence of God to touch us every day. I call it soaking or marinating. More, Lord! We need to allow ourselves to be touched daily by the glory of God. Sometimes I'll wait every day for a whole hour for His presence to come. I'll just lie on the floor and fill up with the Holy Spirit. Spending time with the Holy Spirit soaking in His Presence is crucial to our love relationship with God.

4. Be Redeemed by the Blood of Jesus Christ: "I am dark, but lovely" (Song of Songs 1:5). The Shulammite bride is saying (about herself), that she is dark but lovely. Being dark symbolizes sinful desires. She goes on to say, "Don't look upon me, because I am dark" (v.6). It's as if she is saying, "I am dark. Don't look upon me, don't judge me." There is shame, guilt and condemnation. But the flip side is that she is lovely.

I believe that once Jesus Christ has redeemed us we become lovely (1 Peter 1:18-23).

5. Pursue God First and Foremost: Then in her next breath the bride says, "My mother's sons were angry with me; they made me the keeper of the vineyards, but my own vineyard I have not kept" (Song of Songs 1:6b, emphasis mine). The "vineyard" can represent numerous conditions; for instance, ministry work can sometimes rob us from taking care of our own "vineyard." To paraphrase: "They made me the keeper of the vineyards-ministry. They gave me all this responsibility but I'm burned out. They gave me all this work, all this ministry,

but my own vineyard I have not kept. Because of that, I am ashamed because I'm not looking after my own spiritual life with God. I feel abandoned because somehow the church has rejected me even though I've been working so hard." There is something wrong with this picture! Pursue God. Don't pursue vineyards. God will desire your beauty and He will draw you aside with Him so that He can awaken and renew your "first love" for Him (Revelations 2:4).

6. Rest in God and Be Connected to the Body of Christ: "Tell me, O you whom I love, where you feed your flock, where you make it rest at noon. For why should I be as one who veils herself by the flocks of your companions?" (Song of Songs 1:7). Here we see the bride's earnest desire for him. It's as If she was saying, "Tell me O you whom I love. Even though I am dark and even though I am burned out, I have a hunger for you. Can you please tell me where I can get some revelation? Can you please tell me where you feed your flocks the manna of heaven?" Isn't that the cry of the church today? We want to know the place of revelation even like Job had it-the friendly counsel of God waiting at his tent (Job 29:4). We want to hear the voice of God and have visions, dreams, encounters, experiences and visitations. People have asked me how I receive revelation. They want to know, what book did you read? Hey! I found a place in the spirit where "He feeds His flocks" and I go there.

Here are two keys that reveal where revelation is found. The first is found in Psalm 23:2 "He makes me to lie down in green pastures; He leads me beside the still waters." The second is in Song of Solomon 1:8 "If you do not know, O fairest among women, follow in the footsteps of the flock and feel your little goats beside the shepherds tents." Follow the footsteps of God's people, His flock. Look for the footprints of the: God chasers-those that have prophetic history and destiny. Find out where they walked. Be inspired by the stories of Abraham, Moses, Deborah, Esther and Ruth. Read about other great saints used by God like Smith Wigglesworth, Kathryn Kuhlman, Aimee Semple McPherson and others. Find the footprints of the flock. You see, God wants to give us a revelation and we need the rest of God (Hebrews 4:9-11), as well as being connected into the body of Christ (Hebrews 10:25), beside the shepherd's tent. The revelation of God's love for us arouses out love and passion for Him.

7. Follow the Footsteps: "But imitate those whose faith and patience inherit the promises" (Hebrews 6:12b). Something happens to us when we follow in the footsteps of Jesus. Let us not forget the heroes of the faith from days of old and in modern times. As we imitate or try to be like Jesus and the great men and women of God, our love and passion for God is stirred. Let's not miss the forerunners, the men and women of God who spur us on!

8. Catch the Little Foxes! "Catch is the foxes, the little foxes that spoil the vines, for our vines have tender grapes" (Song of Songs 2:15). If we went to awaken love, we need to catch those little foxes-the subtle areas of our life that distract disturb and hinder us from resting in the secret place. Many believers are not caught up in a big sun but rather there are subtle areas that dull their love for God. I call these little foxes "the intimacy robbers." Intimacy robbers are those conditions that try to make our love for God grow cold. The devil knows how vital it is to rob from us deep intimacy with God.

He knows that in the secret place of intimacy, believers discover the essence of true worship and how our devotion to God causes His heart to be ravished with love for His creation. If the devil's schemes remain uncontested, he can keep us out of the secret place of God's presence by pushing those little foxes into our circumstances.

As our "love-life" with God matures, He is ever mindful of the multitudes of people who are lost and dying. They need to be reached with the gospel by Christians who's hearts are aflame with God's burning love. "Set me as a seal upon you heart, as a seal upon your love is as strong as death. Jealousy as cruel as the grave; it's flames are flames of fire, a most passionate flame" (Song of Songs 8:6). Love-its flames are flames of fire. A most severe flame!

God's fiery seal of supernatural love comes upon our hearts to empower us to love a lost world with the very love that Jesus has. It's a mature, fiery, passionate love, full of flames of fire.

Do your part. Kindle, rekindle, stoke, fan and steward the flame, His fiery, hot, intoxicating love on you today, and to consume you with a holy desperation for one thing only-to know His fullness.

How to Open the Windows of Heaven

Jesus saw heaven open and then the Holy Spirit descended. We have to get the heavens open. Here are a few keys:

My experience of open heavens started with holy hunger. You've got to be hungry for His presence. Ask Him for holy hunger and then press in. You'll see better results from asking God to make you hungry and fervent than you will by trying to muster up your own determination and willpower to make yourself hungry and fervent.

I listen to worship music and just lie on the carpet, meditating and thinking about Jesus. I quiet my mind of all busyness and when it wonders I simply refocus on Jesus. That brings the presence of the Lord. Now I don't even have to press in to get the presence. I can just get into that position and the presence comes. I've become very sensitive. Live out 1 Samuel 3:1-8. I want to be like the boy Samuel and lie where the ark of God is. If the glory is around I want to be quiet and lie in it. There is a place for prayer and praise but mostly we are just trying to worship our way into the presence. It's important to practice the presence.

How do I get an open heaven? Get back into obedience. Repentance opens heaven and obedience keeps it open.

2 Chronicles 7:13, 14 If I shut up heaven that there be no rain, or if I command the locusts to devour the land, or if I send pestilence among my people; If my people, which are called by my name, shall humble themselves, and pray, and seek my face,

and turn from their wicked ways; then will I hear from heaven, and will forgive their sin, and will heal their land.

Notice the first verse: "When I shut up heaven." When heaven is shut there is no blessing, revival, or fruitfulness.

Joel 1:13, 14 Gird yourselves, and lament, ye priests: howl, ye ministers of the altar: come, lie all night in sackcloth, ye ministers of my God: for the meat offering and the drink offering is withholden from the house of your God. Sanctify ye a fast, call a solemn assembly, gather the elders and all the inhabitants of the land into the house of the LORD your God, and cry unto the LORD,

This passage described the church in a terrible place. The abundance was gone; it was dry, the land laid waste, there was no fruit, the fig tree was bare and the harvest of the field had died. No one was getting saved. God had also cut off the new wine-the drink offering. We need to understand that the two most important ingredients to having a relationship with God back then were oil and wine. If they couldn't bring their offerings, then they couldn't receive atonement. When God cut off the new wine and the new oil, He said in effect that His relationship with them was severed. These were people desperately in need of an open heaven. Joel commanded prayer and fasting.

Lie all night at the altar, pray and fast. If there is any area of your life where heaven is shut, fasting and prayer will open it.

When heaven is closed it takes desperate prayer for God to restore as He did for His people in Joel 2:23-25:

Joel 2:23-25 Be glad then, ye children of Zion, and rejoice in the LORD your God: for he hath given you the former rain moderately, and he will cause to come down for you the rain, the former rain, and the latter rain in the first month. And the floors shall be full of wheat, and the fats shall overflow with wine and oil. And I will restore to you the years that the locust hath eaten, the cankerworm, and the caterpiller, and the palmerworm, my great army which I sent among you.

Most people like me the entire time I preach this message until I address this very sensitive area-tithes and offerings.

Extravagant giving is proven throughout Scripture to open the heavens. What does money really have to do with God and the spirit realm? It's amazing how many times God draws a parallel between heaven and blessing and money. Maybe it shows us where our hearts are.

Remember, the love of money is the root of all evil (1 Timothy 6:10).

People think if they tithe they are going to get blessed. I know people who tithe who are not blessed. Do you know why? Because they tithe by the law. Someone might say, "Well tithing is by the law." No it's not. God did it with Abraham before the law. It's by faith. Someone else might argue that there is no tithing in the New Testament. Jesus didn't excuse the tithe, but He did have strong words to say to the teachers of the law and the Pharisees who were tithing without mercy, faithfulness and justice.

Matthew 23:23 Woe unto you, scribes and Pharisees, hypocrites! for ye pay tithe of mint and anise and cummin, and have omitted the weightier matters of the law, judgment, mercy, and faith: these ought ye to have done, and not to leave the other undone.

A reason some faithful givers don't receive blessings is because they are stingy about it. They tithe 10 percent-and that's it. Tithes alone don't open the windows of heaven-tithes and offerings do.

The tithe breaks up the ground so that the rest of the seed (offerings) can bring forth fruit. The Word says in Malachi that when you bring your tithes and offerings into the storehouse, God will open the windows of heaven.

Malachi 3:8-10 Will a man rob God? Yet ye have robbed me. But ye say, Wherein have we robbed thee? In tithes and offerings. Ye are cursed with a curse: for ye have robbed me, even this whole nation. Bring ye all the tithes into the storehouse, that there may be meat in mine house, and prove me now herewith, saith the LORD of hosts, if I will not open you the windows of heaven, and pour you out a blessing, that there shall not be room enough to receive it.

In Deuteronomy 28:12 the Lord called His storehouse "the heavens." Is it possible to take my money and put it in His good treasure-the heavens? God said, "I am going to open up the windows of heaven to pour out blessings."

We always use this verse to refer to money, but it really includes all the benefits of the open heaven: "The LORD will open to you His good treasure, the heavens, to give the rain to your land in its season and to bless all the work of your hand. You shall lend too many nations, but you shall not borrow."

In the second chapter of Acts, God opened the heavens and poured out His Spirit; three thousand souls were saved, the church emerged and immediately people sold their land, houses and laid their offerings at the apostles' feet. Generosity and extravagant giving were released. Do you believe that God is your Provider? Would you like to operate in the heavenly system so that you are not affected by the economy? I would much rather bank through a heavenly ATM. If I want my money to be in that heavenly system, I have to put my money where that system is.

Get the Word into your heart, mind and soul daily.

You will find powerful insights into living a life of daily intimacy with God through meditating on God.

People often ask me: Why did God pick Litchfield, IL, for the tremendous outpouring of healings and miracles you were involved in? What was it about that small church? God chose Litchfield because the people there believed that they could open the heavens through servant evangelism. Servant evangelism opens heaven over cities and towns. I was being moved to minister to the lost.

Galatians 5:6 For in Jesus Christ neither circumcision availeth any thing, nor uncircumcision; but faith which worketh by love.

Galatians 5:13 For, brethren, ye have been called unto liberty; only use not liberty for an occasion to the flesh, but by love serve one another.

Love acts. Love never fails. Faith works through love.

For a change, let's forget power evangelism, prophetic evangelism, preaching on the street corners and tracts.

Let's show God's love by action. Buy someone groceries. Head on down to a skateboard park and buy the gang hotdogs. Give out gas vouchers, mow lawns, or wash cars for free. It will open heaven because faith will bring wonders and power.

Jesus was moved with compassion and He healed every sickness and disease. If you want to get more of God's power in your life, try some acts of compassion. The Bible says to bless your enemies. Try doing something nice for them that would blow their minds.

There is a River

There is a River, the streams whereof shall make glad the city of God, the holy place of the tabernacles of the most High. God is in the midst of her; she shall not be moved: God shall help her and that right early. Psalms 46:4-5

Ezekiel 47:3-5 And when the man that had the line in his hand went forth eastward, he measured a thousand cubits, and he brought me through the waters; the waters were to the ankles. Again he measured a thousand, and brought me through the waters; the waters were to the knees. Again he measured a thousand, and brought me through; the waters were to the loins. Afterward he measured a thousand; and it was a river that I could not pass over: for the waters were risen, waters to swim in, a river that could not be passed over.

John 7:37-39 In the last day, that great day of the feast, Jesus stood and cried, saying, If any man thirst, let him come unto me, and drink. He that believeth on me, as the scripture hath said, out of his belly shall flow rivers of living water. (But this spake he of the Spirit, which they that believe on him should receive: for the Holy Ghost was not yet given; because that Jesus was not yet glorified.)

Revelations 22:1 And he shewed me a pure river of water of life, clear as crystal, proceeding out of the throne of God and of the Lamb.

Isaiah 43:18-21 Remember ye not the former things, neither consider the things of old. Behold, I will do a new thing; now it shall spring forth; shall ye not know it? I will even make a way in the wilderness, and rivers in the desert. The beast of the field shall honour me, the dragons and the owls: because I give waters in the wilderness, and rivers in the desert, to give drink to my people, my chosen. This people have I formed for myself; they shall shew forth my praise.

This is a prophetic Chapter releasing Rivers of Glory.

I give waters in the wilderness and rivers in the desert.... Wait no longer; the river is here. For many years the church has prayed and anxiously awaited another wave of heavenly glory that would lift us out of spiritual stupor and surround us with the presence and power of the living God that has been demonstrated in past revivals. Well, the wait is over. God is moving by His Spirit all over the world and all we have to do is step into the revival. The river is here. Something wonderful is happening. We are conscious of standing in the waters of a heavenly stream. Some of us have taken only small steps away from the shoreline, but many of us are finding ourselves in deeper and deeper water without having to put forth any effort whatsoever. The river is carrying us out. It's here. It is no longer difficult for us to move from the ankle-deep water into the knee-deep water and from the knee-deep water into the loin-deep water.

It is somehow easy now to move on out into even deeper places, into water to swim in. All we need to do is yield to the river and the river does the work. What we are experiencing is so wonderful that sometimes it seems more like a dream than reality. Recently, when I am in special meetings, it seems almost as if my arms don't belong to me. They feel very strange as the Lord possesses them to use for His glory. I sometimes seem to be looking down or looking on as I see what God is doing with my life and for the people. These are wonderful days to be alive.

The river is here. God is doing new things and I like that. God is doing things differently than we could have anticipated. He is sending revival in His own way and is calling for a people who will accept revival on His terms.

When the river of God's Spirit is flowing, it doesn't matter who the speaker is. God does the work. Now people come because they want to be in the atmosphere of the glory. If the glory of God is present, nothing else matters. The river is here. We have not been able to predict exactly how God would bring revival to any specific area.

Stop clinging to the shoreline. I know we are afraid of the unknown, but there is no reason to fear God. Let Him carry you away from the realm of your natural thinking. Let Him carry you away into the depths of the river. These waters will carry you to the place of miracles, signs and wonders.

There are many things that God wants to do for us in the depths of the river which we will not be able to analyze. We must just accept them.

Some believers are seriously thinking about leaving the churches they have been attending because they are tired of waiting for revival to come. This, however, is not the time to leave. The river is rising. When you get in touch with the river of God, the first thing you notice is how enormous it is. It only takes a few measurements from Heaven to quickly get you in over your head and you suddenly find yourself swimming. It doesn't take long at all to realize that this river has no boundaries, no limits and we are only beginning to explore the vastness of it.

There is a broadness to this river that none of us has yet perceived and we can only perceive it as we allow God to take us out into it. Cooperate with Him.

Revelations 22:1 And he shewed me a pure river of water of life, clear as crystal, proceeding out of the throne of God and of the Lamb.

Any time you get into God's river, you are standing at the Source. That is why we are called to focus our attention on the river. This river of God can never be changed. It is pure because its Source is pure. No man can contaminate it with interpretation or bias. No man can twist it to his own liking, to fit his own patterns. There is life and power in the river and if we apply the healing power of its waters we would have a greater quality of life. Learn to come to the Lord's river first. The greatest miracles take place in an atmosphere of great worship and great liberty. If we desire to see great miracles, we must gather together in simplicity, praise the Lord until the spirit of worship comes and worship Him until the glory comes.

Whatever is touched by the river will live. Every part of your being will come alive in God and there will be no death in you. No part of your being will be unwell. Through the work of the river, you will be experiencing a glorious healing flow. We are only just beginning to tap into the power of the river of God. In it is an endless supply of all the power we need. How do you reap a worldwide harvest? How do you organize a worldwide revival? We don't have to worry about it. The Guide, the Teacher is with us.

God's desire is to take us places we can't ask to be taken because we don't know they even exist. He wants to give us experiences that we could never request because we have never yet even dreamed of them. When you are in the presence of God, resist the temptation to think about your plans for tomorrow, next week or next year. Live in the moment, that eternal moment in God. Don't expect Him to show you what you want; let Him show you what He wants. He is the Guide.

There are ever-greater depths for us to explore, but the Spirit Himself goes with us and is the One to measure everything for us. There is no reason for fear.

Those who have never been to other countries need to get their traveling shoes ready and their suitcases packed. At some point in this revival God will give many the privilege of standing on foreign soil to help gather in the harvest from among the nations. No nation and no denomination within individual nations will remain untouched by the revival. God will pour out His Spirit as we have never seen it before. This revival will go far beyond churches. Not a single government organization or department will be untouched by it. The river will seep in through every crack. There will be no way to keep it out of every government building.

God always chooses the Litchfield's and the little places of this world. He chooses the Smithton's. It is because He does not want anyone to glorify the place rather than the river.

In the flow of the river of God, you experience a defining moment, catching a glimpse, often for the very first time, of the purpose of your life. Healing for the nations seems like a lofty goal, a difficult thing to believe for, but after Ezekiel had seen it with his own eyes, it was not only easy to believe for, but it also became easy for him to declare. Unless we allow the river of God to affect our seeing, we can accomplish little for His

Kingdom. There has always been revelation in the river of God, but we are about to see a release of revelation beyond anything we have known before. In that greater revelatory realm, we will see and speak the very mysteries of God. God has called us to be a people of knowing. We should not always have to wait so long to get His leading for every major decision. Sometimes we don't have time for another forty-day fast. It is time to walk in the Spirit of revelation.

The Holy Spirit is the Initiator, He drops the thought into our spirit and those holy thoughts that are dropped into our spirits are called revelations. They didn't emanate from us; they emanated from Him.

They are the thoughts of the Lord at a given moment, the mind of Christ in action. Promotion in the Kingdom of God comes directly from the King Himself. The Lord has new positions for each of us and because of the rapid growth in the Church, this is promotion time. While you may insist that you have no gift of this caliber, you will never know until you get it unwrapped. That's the way gifts are. We can stand in the place God has put us in the depths of the river and receive a gift of the Spirit that will call a nation. The river doesn't wait for anybody. When something is flowing downstream and we want to catch it, we have to act fast or we may miss it.

For those who step boldly into God's waters, a worldwide calling awaits. Because of our human limitations, it requires a miracle for us to even contain God's vision. In the flow of the river, He gives us an enlargement of heart that enables us to carry the vision that He has placed within us. Rise to the occasion. In the flow of the river, there is promotion. Every limitation that men would try to put upon us is taken away.

GLORY: EXPANDING GOD'S PRESENCE: DISCOVER HOW TO MANIFEST GOD'S GLORY

When we are willing to take hold of the vision of the Lord, it is amazing how God opens doors for us, doors that no man can shut. There is no limitation in the Spirit. There is no limitation in the glory. Those who dwell on the positive and confess the positive will be raised up overnight with special anointings that will amaze and confound the world. Some people sit down and try to plan it and while they are busy with the details of how they will get it done, God has already used the person next to them to accomplish the goal.

WHENCE THEN COMETH WISDOM? AND WHERE IS THE PLACE OF UNDERSTANDING?

GOD UNDERSTANDETH THE WAY THEREOF, AND HE KNOWETH THE PLACE THEREOF.

There is no need for us to search out the wisdom we require. God has already found it. There is no need for us to seek the right way. He already knows the way.

Our God is wisdom and understanding and the more we know Him in this holy dimension of His glory, the greater our understanding will be for the revival of these last days. This river is filled with wisdom and if you are found in its waters, God's wisdom will be found in you. Now the LORD had said unto Abram, Get thee out of thy country and from thy kindred and from thy father's house, unto a land that I will show thee: AND I WILL MAKE OF THEE A GREAT NATION, AND I WILL BLESS THEE AND MAKE THY NAME GREAT; AND THOU SHALT BE A BLESSING: And I will bless them that bless thee and curse him that curseth thee: and in thee shall all families of the earth be blessed. Genesis 12:1-3

Whether our ancestors came over on the Mayflower or whether our being an American is the result of some of the more modern calls sent forth by God to other lands and people, we are all here because someone responded to the voice of the Holy Spirit to become part of a new and great nation.

If people could only realize that when they are slain in the Spirit they are falling into greatness, surely they would fall down more often. That which is happening in our services is a transaction between Heaven and Earth. Let fireballs from the Holy Spirit roll forth from your hands to do the work. Let sparks of fire come forth from your mouth so that your words will be effective. I have watched it happen through the years. When people get into the river, they are suddenly dreaming great dreams, having great visions and exploring glorious plans. This present revival will not only touch the soul. It will be an economic revival for God's people. We will not only get out of debt, but we will receive outstanding financial miracles for our every need. Those who lack will miraculously be given what they need to meet their financial obligations and those who have surpluses will be called upon to place some of their surplus into the Kingdom. This is not a day for exclusivity. This is not a day to maintain separations. God is removing them all. Labels are falling off. Barriers are coming down. Offenses are being forgotten.

Our independent spirits must flee away and we must reach out, taking one another by the hand and move together, as waves of the glory of God wash over us. In the uniting of our hands, suddenly the individual flows were merged into one great flow. Rather than two separate flows, we now had one. God wants to send forth rivers of living waters from our innermost being, but we must remove the dams. We can no longer allow bitterness, envy, or strife to hinder the flow of the river of God. We cannot afford to allow anything that other people say or do to us to hinder that flow. It is not a time to concern ourselves with minors. Let us stick to the majors. If we get caught up in the struggle over small things, we might miss what God is doing. When the river is flowing in us and we are flowing in the river, we will no longer ask each other about denominational background or affiliation. It is not relevant. In the days to come, we will not just harvest individual fish, but entire schools of fish will be taken.

In every way possible, God is letting us know that the harvest we will see in this last day will surpass the measurements we have grown accustomed to using. This harvest will not be a struggle. This harvest will not be reaped by the sweat of our brow. Fish will be harvested because of the waters of the river and for no other reason. When we become conscious that a miracle flow is present, we can just jump into the river and receive the miracle of healing we need. In the flow of the river there are miracles for your body, for your ministry, for your finances. There are miracles for your children you don't have to make it happen. Just get into the flow and the miracles will be there. We will see greater and greater things as the day's progress. In this river there is a flow of healing capable of touching every nation of the Earth and no nation will remain untouched by it in the days ahead. Our God is a God of miracles, a God of the unusual, a God of the impossible. Don't try to tell Him how to do it. The river is here and there is healing in its life-giving flow, the flow of River Glory.

As we move forward into revival, we can also expect many and varied signs from Heaven. I have observed that when we see something unusual happen suddenly to others, we doubt its authenticity. When it happens to us, however, we are immediately sure it is of God. These experiences have taught me not to make judgments about where people are in their Christian experience. God is bringing people into new realms. When we are caught away in the river, we are taken out of the realm of our own reasoning and brought into God's realm, where we become totally dependent upon Him. Because we have been afraid of the unknown, we have only begun to see what God can do for us. He desires to carry us out so quickly into the depths that we will look at one another in amazement. Nothing will be impossible to us in the days ahead as we move further into River Glory. How could we as people of the river possibly be concerned about the waters of adversity that are coming our way? We know that there is a river and that is enough. God is looking for a people who will not be embarrassed with victory. His people have no need to look as if they need a handout.

They don't need to have the appearance of those who have suffered many afflictions. This river of God must be glimpsed by revelation and laid hold of by faith. Let us journey to it, pitch our tent beside it and jump in. If you have to go through some valleys to get to the next high place, don't worry about it. You are still higher than you were before. You are still moving forward. In the river there is an abundant supply of anything you can name, all that you will ever need. You can never contain this river and you can never control it. You can only present yourself as a willing channel for its flow. You be the river bed. Let the river of life flow through you and your bed will become greatly enlarged.

The Lord Himself sets the pattern and that is why we must listen to the voice of the Spirit of God as He is speaking to us in our services. When the river is flowing, there is liberty and if liberty is lacking, we know that the river is not present or that it is not being allowed to flow.

No one need be afraid of this invitation. If the Lord says to you, I'll meet you in the river You are not going home now. He is just quickening you, anointing you, revitalizing you, enduing you with power from on high, putting a newness into your spirit, a newness into your walk, a newness into your talk, a newness into your life, so that you can rise up and do exploits.

God is doing new things in the river. He is performing miracles. He is bringing signs and wonders forth by the power of His Holy Spirit and He is inviting you to participate. Don't be concerned about getting out too deep. Be concerned about not getting out deep enough. When we get among people who are all swimming, we say to ourselves, what am I doing here, just splashing my feet in the water, when I could be swimming in the depth of the river too?. It makes us willing to get out there and swim with them. It is not enough that the river is here. If you don't step into its waters, you will not benefit from its life-giving flow. The act of stepping into the water, therefore, is of utmost importance.

God is doing whatever it takes to free us quickly. What used to take many years, as we progressed through all the spiritual stages, is now being done in a very short time through the work of the Spirit. He is giving us a total immersion process. No part of us is excluded. Most rivers flow in only one direction, but don't expect the same of the river of life. One time it will flow in one direction and the next time in another. The important thing is not to understand how the river flows but to get in and flow with it whatever direction it is flowing at the moment. There is, within the souls of God's people these days, a greater and greater hunger for the things of His Spirit. This hunger will not allow us to rest in the shallow places. It is urging us to let go of the shore and be carried out into greater things. Sometimes God has to allow something to knock us off our feet so that we can get out into the depths of the river and learn to flow with it. We can talk about faith and preach about faith, but when we get into the depths of the river, we will suddenly know faith. How can we just stand on the shore when others are already getting into deeper waters?

How can we afford to refuse to jump in when others are enjoying the benefits of the river? If you want to see the miracle flow, launch out into the deep. There is something about the new song that brings a release in ways that nothing else can. The move of the Spirit of God comes on the wings of song and as some of you release your song to the Lord you will find yourself flowing in a new dimension of the Spirit, soaring in a new realm of the Spirit, moving to a new place in God. I can say that the new song has enriched my life in ways that nothing else, other than vision, has. The new song can open the treasure chests of Heaven and pour forth riches from our own mouths.

While we are worshipping Him in the steps of the dance, the Lord is working changes within us and fine-tuning us to come into step with the realms of His glory. He is placing Heaven's tempo, Heaven's rhythm and Heaven's responses deep within our beings.

When we reach out in the Spirit for new words and music with which to worship our Lord, suddenly there is a release of His Spirit that comes into our midst and wonderful things happen. When we dance before the Lord, much more is being accomplished than most of us could ever imagine. While we are worshipping Him in the steps of the dance, the Lord is working changes within us and fine-tuning us to come into step with the realms of His glory.

There are times that we need to rejoice in the fact that the Lord is King. We can rejoice in His presence and rejoice in what He is doing.

Jeremiah 33:11 The voice of joy, and the voice of gladness, the voice of the bridegroom, and the voice of the bride, the voice of them that shall say, Praise the LORD of hosts: for the LORD is good; for his mercy endureth for ever: and of them that shall bring the sacrifice of praise into the house of the LORD. For I will cause to return the captivity of the land, as at the first, saith the LORD.

When laughter wells up within us, I am convinced that God is enlarging our river beds and making room for a greater flow of His Spirit. There are things that we must give voice to. They are there; we just need to let them out. Laugh your way right into the depths of the river. Desire makes people travel long distances to receive God's touch upon their lives. It causes them to push aside the nonessentials so that they can have God's best. It is not enough that the river comes down from Heaven. It is not enough that it is in the church or in the conference or in the revival center. God wants it to flow through you. Until it is coming forth from your innermost being, He is not satisfied.

When you stop drinking, the river stops flowing. Once we have experienced the river, we can no longer be satisfied with anything else. No artificial waters can quench our thirst. No substitute will meet our need. Revival is here. Drink deeply. It is not enough to drink once. We must drink and drink and drink and drink some more. The river itself suddenly takes over and we find ourselves being carried away by the greatness of it.

While you are struggling so hard to stay connected, God is doing everything He can to get you unconnected. When the river is present, you don't necessarily need to preach about it. Just let it flow. It is not always necessary to point it out and tell people to get in. Just let if flow. You get in and others will follow you.

A Day of Open Doors

This is the day which God hath made; We will rejoice and be glad in it—Psalms 118:24

This is a day of destiny that the Lord has made! We have crossed a threshold in heavens time-line. The Bible calls it the "fullness of time." The apostle Paul in his epistle to the Galatians stated,

Galatians 4:4-6 But when the fulness of the time was come, God sent forth his Son, made of a woman, made under the law, To redeem them that were under the law, that we might receive the adoption of sons. And because ye are sons, God hath sent forth the Spirit of his Son into your hearts, crying, Abba, Father.

The central theme of our revelations highlights our position in modern church history and prophetic destiny in God. We are biblically promised a generation who will be:

1. The Greater Works Generation-—John 14:12
2. The Plum-line/Capstone Generation-—Zechariah 4
3. The Restoration of All Things Generation—Hebrews 6:5
4. The Righteous Generation-—Psalms 14
5. The Generation Who Will Seek His Face-—Psalms 24
6. The Latter Rain Generation-—Joel 2
7. The Brides Revival Generation-—John 20:21
8. The Mature Sons of the Kingdom-—Matthew 13
9. The Third Day Generation-—Hosea 6:2

10. The Fullness Generation-—Ephesians 4:13

These will be the "sons of the Kingdom" who carry the Sevenfold Spirit of God that rested upon the Lord Himself in His perfect example of a Son of the Kingdom.

This is a day in which many promises will be apprehended and divine destiny achieved. Over the past several years there have been messages of preparation sounded as a clarion call to the Bride of Christ to prepare for the coming battle. Those individuals who have heeded this call and allowed the sifting and pruning process will begin to emerge with considerable anointing and authority. For them, this will be a day of substantial advancement

Throughout biblical history we can see God's hand taking His servants through various trials and character molding journeys. The design is to bring them out on the other side with the revelation of His nature. Though the passage may at times seem difficult, it is for our benefit in order to steward faithfully God's provision.

The time for the apprehension of promises is now upon us.

The Bible clearly outlines that every good and perfect gift comes from the Father of Lights. God is Light and in Him there is no shifting shadow. Consequently, we are likewise called to be light in the midst of a dark generation.

It was by His own will that he gave us birth as "sons of the Kingdom" by His Word of Truth. We are designated to be a form of first fruits of His creation and a representation of what the "sons of the Kingdom" are called and consecrated to be.

Through his epistle to the Ephesians, the apostle Paul admonishes us to conduct ourselves as children of light. He said,

Ephesians 5:7-10 Be not ye therefore partakers with them. For ye were sometimes darkness, but now are ye light in the Lord: walk as children of light: (For the fruit of the Spirit is in all goodness and righteousness and truth;) Proving what is acceptable unto the Lord.

The surest evidence of the "Children of Light" and God's true leadership will be the clear presence of the fruit of the Spirit. God's righteousness will begin to reflect the Spirit's nature in our lives. The display of His character in us is ultimately pleasing to the Lord and the reflection of His Light that we must possess.

Matthew 13:37-39 He answered and said unto them, He that soweth the good seed is the Son of man; The field is the world; the good seed are the children of the kingdom; but the tares are the children of the wicked one; The enemy that sowed them is the devil; the harvest is the end of the world; and the reapers are the angels.

If we are to be the "light" of the world, we will possess qualities consistent with "sons of the Kingdom" and children of light by allowing Christ to be fully manifested in us. The identification, anointing and purpose of this company who overcomes are listed below.

1. Their Identification-The manifestation of the Fruit of the Spirit - Galatians 5:22-24

2. Their Anointing-—The Seven Spirits of God- Isaiah 11:2

3. Their Purpose - To reveal the twelve names illustrating the divine character of God and His primary redemptive attributes manifested in the Person of Jesus.

The Lord is indicating His desire to restore through His church, His original mandate for man and fully heal the breach that has existed since man's fall in the garden. Our cities will reflect Heaven's light only to the degree that the saints within them do.

Matthew 5:14-16 Ye are the light of the world. A city that is set on an hill cannot be hid. Neither do men light a candle, and put it under a bushel, but on a candlestick; and it giveth light unto all that are in the house. Let your light so shine before men, that they may see your good works, and glorify your Father which is in heaven.

One of the primary strategies to win our cities is through unity of the brethren.

If the Lord can find just a few willing to live together in harmony with a common cause of advancing God's Kingdom, then He will pour out a special anointing of grace and favor that will illuminate our dwelling places. We will have unity to the degree that Christ is formed in us.

When this takes place we will then carry the battle to enemy gates and invade our cities with the ministry of restoration and awakening. We will help those who once experienced failure find their rightful place in the body of

Christ. We will also retrieve those of our brethren who have fallen and begin to rejuvenate them into a new walk with Christ while also rescuing the unbelieving from the snare of the evil one.

The Lord recently expressed His desire to deal with the strongholds in us so we can deal with the strongholds in our churches, cities and nation. The Holy Spirit spoke to me in a meeting and said "If the people will allow Me to remove the stumbling-blocks **within** them, I will then remove the ones **before** them."

God's people are called to be the repairers of the breach and restorers of streets and dwellings. Isaiah 58:12 declares,

Isaiah 58:12 And they that shall be of thee shall build the old waste places: thou shalt raise up the foundations of many generations; and thou shalt be called, The repairer of the breach, The restorer of paths to dwell in.

In order to do that effectively in our cities, the Lord is sending "angels that gather" His Kingdom all things offensive to Him so that He can reflect His Light through us.

Our churches and cities will exhibit Heaven's Light to the extent that the righteous within them do.

The Lord promised that,

Matthew 13:41-43 The Son of man shall send forth his angels, and they shall gather out of his kingdom all things that offend, and them which do iniquity; And shall cast them into a furnace of fire: there shall be wailing and gnashing of teeth. Then shall the righteous shine forth as the sun in the kingdom of their Father. Who hath ears to hear, let him hear.

The Bible tells us that the Kingdom of Heaven is within us. The righteous will shine like the sun in the Kingdom of our Father when the tares and stumbling blocks have been extracted from our soul. Light dispels the darkness of our soul as He lights the candle of our innermost being.

The Lord clothes Himself in light as with a virtuous garment to depict His great authority in Heaven and in creation.

We are likewise called to be endowed with the raiment of light that proceeds from Him. We are summoned to be the light and salt of the earth.

The pure white light of Heaven will proceed from the Throne to be imparted into the spirit and soul of the Lord's people to make us divine carriers of His virtue. Many will encounter the Lights of Heaven in private worship and in corporate settings in amplified ways over the coming months and years. This Light will manifest as the Sevenfold Spirit of God in the same way that pure white light directed through a prism highlights the seven colors of the spectrum.

This is the day that individuals will begin to walk in the light of revelation they possess. There must be an experiential quality to our walk with the Lord. Not only do we experience Him in a tangible way, but also in practical ways that radiate the spiritual Light that has been deposited within us.

This is the model for the lost to be drawn to the Kingdom of Light; then the masses will be drawn to our light and fulfill the prophecies of Daniel when he said,

Daniel 12:3 And they that be wise shall shine as the brightness of the firmament; and they that turn many to righteousness as the stars for ever and ever.

We have now crossed a threshold into the place where we begin to do what we have for so long talked about. This is especially true in the Western Church. This is the day of Lights or the day that people began to walk in the Light of Heaven.

We as a generation have come to a "fullness of time" crossroad in God's plan of progressive restoration. We are assigned the ministry of recovery and reconciliation and the next installment is at the door. It will be marked by notable expression of power with emphasis on the recovery of sight to the blind. It will take place in the natural to indicate a spiritual reality.

Matthew 9:29 Then He touched their eyes, saying, According to your faith and trust and reliance [on the power invested in Me] be it done to you. Amplified

The job of the righteous will be to redeem that which the enemy has stolen and re-dig wells that once flourished with God's healing virtue. The Lord is going to touch blind eyes and execute the recovery of sight both naturally and spiritually.

We will especially be called to recover and heal those who have been wounded in the church. The "blind, lame and halt" are to be revitalized by those developing in righteousness; thereby retaking ground previously relented to the enemy.

Even the gifts of the Spirit that have been stolen or perverted by the enemy will be redeemed during the coming year and years to follow.

The righteous must begin to restore all of these things the enemy has successfully stolen or perverted within the church, especially the ministry of healing.

Highlighted revelatory truth is being set before us through words that are not taught by human wisdom, but by the Holy Spirit. It is the consolidation of spiritual truth with spiritual language in and through those possessing the Spirit of

Understanding. There are corporate and personal messages proceeding from God's heart relative to our destiny and position in Heaven's economy. Paul said,

1 Corinthians 2:12, 13 Now we have received, not the spirit of the world, but the spirit which is of God; that we might know the things that are freely given to us of God. Which things also we speak, not in the words which man's wisdom teacheth, but which the Holy Ghost teacheth; comparing spiritual things with spiritual.

Having the understanding that the Lord is grooming us for something significant transforms our mind-set and generates hope to displace hopelessness.

Without this comprehension we would indeed experience profound hopelessness and despair. A double portion restoration and return is our legacy.

Our council is to cooperate with heaven and do only what we see the Father doing and say only what we hear Him saying. The Lord is opening our eyes and ears with the Spirit of Understanding so that our discernment is taken to greater levels to accomplish this purpose.

There has been a sifting of our soul and the establishment of contrition, humility and meekness in order to carry greater levels of power and authority. The Spirit of Understanding will bring illumination to this reality and mobilize God's people for this great task.

Kindness and truth are indispensable powerful ingredients necessary in God's formula to awaken this generation. (Proverbs 3:3-4)

The Holy Spirit has been punctuating this reality in recent days. If we embody and convey the Lord's meekness we will also share in His power; if we share in His obedience we will also share is His resurrection

The Spirits of Wisdom and Revelation entrusted to us have been unfolding spiritual blueprints and strategies for this day. Many intercessory groups and ministries have seen these outlines and sown revelatory prayer for their fulfillment. The prophetic day they foresaw is now upon us. This day will be like the one Ezekiel spoke,

Ezekiel 12:21-25 And the word of the LORD came unto me, saying, Son of man, what is that proverb that ye have in the land of Israel, saying, The days are prolonged, and every vision faileth? Tell them therefore, Thus saith the Lord GOD; I will make this proverb to cease, and they shall no more use it as a proverb in Israel; but say unto them, The days are at hand, and the effect of every vision. For there shall be no more any vain vision nor flattering divination within the house of Israel. For I am the LORD: I will speak, and the word that I shall speak shall come to pass; it shall be no more prolonged: for in your days, O rebellious house, will I say the word, and will perform it, saith the Lord GOD.

Over the past season many prophetic proclamations and decrees have gone forth. However, we have seen little in the way of significant fulfillment. However, that trend is now changing.

As it was with the prophecies of Ezekiel, so shall it be today. No longer will the proverb be spoken that the visions linger and their fulfillment is delayed. We will now begin to see a more sure word of prophecy emerging that will be accomplished.

The scriptures plainly points out, the Lord ever lives to make intercession on our behalf and if there was ever a time to draw near to God, it is this generation. The Lord is continuing to ask the church to join Him in His heart of intercession for this prophetic generation. When we do, our prophetic decrees will be more accurate because they are generated from the Lord's heart.

He will put a word in our mouths to,

Jeremiah 1:10-12 See, I have this day set thee over the nations and over the kingdoms, to root out, and to pull down, and to destroy, and to throw down, to build, and to plant. Moreover the word of the LORD came unto me, saying, Jeremiah, what seest thou? And I said, I see a rod of an almond tree. Then said the LORD unto me, Thou hast well seen: for I will hasten my word to perform it.

Clearly we are living in a day when miracles, signs and wonders are an essential aspect of our New Testament heritage. (Romans 15:18-19) As in the early church, God's healing power and extraordinary exploits provide Heaven's validation necessary to meet the great needs of the masses.

Our message must be confirmed with the miraculous to be most effective. However, the greatest application will be the spiritual awakening of God's people to receive spiritual eyes to see and ears to hear.

We must alleviate the mistakes of the past and recognize our day of visitation.

After 40 years of governing the people of Israel while in the wilderness, Moses came to the end of the journey and provided a revealing discovery that prohibited that generation from entering the promise. He admonished them with a rehearsal of the great awesome deeds (actions) and demonstrations of the Lord's power performed in their midst. Nonetheless, Moses also pointed out a sad reality- that generation did not receive the promise because, he said,

Deuteronomy 29:4 Yet the LORD hath not given you an heart to perceive, and eyes to see, and ears to hear, unto this day.

What a great lesson for us to learn in our day. Although we can witness notable expressions of spiritual power and authority, that in itself is not enough. It remains essential for us to receive an impartation from the Holy Spirit to possess eyes & ears open to His truth and hearts of understanding.

Without that spiritual endowment, we cannot enter the fullness of the promise.

Not only do we have an inheritance in Him, but He also has an inheritance in us. Our spiritual eyes & ears must be opened to facilitate that union.

It is an important spiritual mandate to have enlightened eyes to see where we are presently placed in human history and the unfolding of God's redemptive plan. Equally as important are gifted eyes that can see ahead to our prophetic destination. From this perspective we can set our sights on the goal of our faith, as well as recognizing the snares and traps of the enemy intended to hinder our ability to get there.

On one unique occasion the prophet Elisha, who had spiritual insight as to where he was and where he was going, boldly stood before the armies of the king of Aram. He could do so because of the spirit of wisdom and revelation that rested upon his life. When his servant nervously recited what his natural eyes were seeing, the prophet prayed, "O LORD, I pray, open his eyes that he may see."

And the LORD opened the servant's eyes and he saw; behold, the mountain was full of horses and chariots of fire all around Elisha

With that prayer, an impartation of spiritual sight was given to the servant. Through that blessing, he discovered with his spiritual eyes, the armies of Heaven and chariots of fire that surrounded God's servant. (2 Kings 6:17-18)

With spiritual vision, fear is replaced with faith and a comprehension of the reality that there are more for us than for the enemy. Nothing changed in this scenario except the vision of Elisha's servant. Without question, his faith level soared. His countenance and courage was not merely based upon the things his natural eyes were seeing, but now his spiritual eyes provided clarity to the entire picture. The same is true today! Supernatural revelation will take us out of rounds of fear and anxiety into the dimensions of God's faith.

The Cloud is Touching Down

At the beginning of last year the Lord began to speak to me about the start of a reformation that was coming to the Body of Christ through a crazy and ecstatic movement of believers that would embrace the wild things of His Kingdom. Over the past year we have seen much change as many are catching a hold of their identity, union and the power of the indwelling of Christ. There is not a day that goes by that I don't meet a person who is so drunk on this message that it spills out of them like a flood.

Especially new believers that have given their lives to Jesus over the past few years and this message has become their daily drink and for this I am truly grateful, since so many long time believers still haven't gotten a hold of, "it is finished". With this message comes greater boldness to declare and demonstrate the power of the gospel and many are beginning to understand that it is not them, but Christ in them demonstrating the power. So with great joy they are releasing the power of Christ without effort all over the world. We are truly living in awesome days and I am excited to see what is ahead for our generation. We have gone so far out that we can't go back. A fresh reformation is upon us and the way we position and posture ourselves will determine the lasting impact we have on the body of Christ in the days ahead. The Cloud is Touching Down with that being said I want to share with you an encounter that I had a few weeks ago that really tilted my grid and shifted my paradigm for what I believe God is asking from us in this hour. During a time of prayer I was taken into a trance and suddenly a flash of light streaked into the living room where I was sitting.

I believe that we are at a very critical time in our generation as revelation is being released from heaven on us and many of these reformers and revivalists are coming out of the cloud of witnesses to release their portion to this generation. If there is one thing we can learn from the life and ministry of a man like the great one's it is this, a true reformation takes time and doesn't come without a price. You must be willing to give everything despite the outcome in the end. What we must understand is the weight of our words and our decisions will determine the legacy that we leave behind for those to follow. The truth is our actions affect so many people more than we realize and the way that we go about causing change within the Body of Christ must not be taken lightly if we truly want to affect generations to come with the message that God has entrusted us with. So often when truth comes that brings freedom we think that people will embrace it whole heartily and change immediately, but it almost never happens that way.

People say they love change, but the truth of the matter is they only like it when it fits into their understanding and structures they've created. When something comes along that literally undoes teachings that have been set in place for 100s of years we can't expect everyone to embrace it immediately, but understand that time is on our side. The pioneers of the past opposed the church on several issues, but was willing to try to work and explain their positions to the leadership within the church at the cost of their reputation and life. We must be willing to do the same. So many times the easiest thing to do is leave; start our own thing, criticize and then lash out at church leaders when they fail to understand the truth that we can so easily see. The true test of a reformer is when you are willing to put your life on the line for what you believe and stand and take the reproach in front of the council. Reformation is defined as the action or process of reforming an institution or practice.

Everything that Christ paid for comes without a "process", but reformation still has one and if we really love Christ and His Church we will be willing to take the journey that so many other reformers did even if that means we will get burned in the end. I believe that God is calling us to reformation from the inside out, not the other way around. And we must be willing to work with those that may, at times, misunderstand us even persecute us if we want to see this message reach beyond a small stream of people and go to the ends of the earth. I am willing to take the chance despite the cost. Will you?

Revival Glory

The glory of God is bringing revival and if we want more revival we must make room for the glory. This is the greatest need of the hour. Our failure to make room for the glory in our services is the most common reason that the glory is not seen and experienced in church after church across America and around the world. I believe that most of the necessary elements are in place, but we simply don't give God a chance. We don't make room for Him to work. We don't make room for the glory. It is not for us to say how the glory will affect us. We must make room for God to do in us what He wants. Prophecy is the voice of revival. Let your prophetic voice bring forth the revival. You'll save yourself thousands of hours of vain activities. Revival is bringing an acceleration of the purposes of God in the Earth and an important part of the revival is the revealing to us of our Bridegroom.

If you have been sidetracked by trying a particular method that has borne fruit for someone else, turn back to find the Lord's presence. He is more important than a method, a system, or a program. Come back to the simplicity of His presence. Under the cloud is the only place of safety. It is the only place of divine health. It is the only place of guaranteed provision. It is the only place of sure revelation. It is the only place which guarantees us salvation for our households and our nation. When you discover things that seem to contribute to the glory, do those things more and when you find things that seem to diminish the glory, stop doing them. It's as simple as that. What hinders us is rarely something complicated. We don't have major problems that need to be overcome, but minor adjustments that need to be made. It is through the revelation of the Spirit that you will be elevated. What God wants to do in these last days can only be accomplished in the glory realm. God's presence is the glory. Revival is spontaneous and we must learn to be spontaneous.

There is a rhythm to the glory and when we speak of the glory cloud, we speak of moving. Ordinary people are seeing things that only great people knew of in days gone by.

I speak revival fire, glory fire, into the souls of all who read this. I declare such a stirring up within, a stirring up unto revival and the taking hold of the same with all that is within and that we will not let go until revival is in our land.

1 Corinthians 1:26-29 For ye see your calling, brethren, how that not many wise men after the flesh, not many mighty, not many noble, are called: But God hath chosen the foolish things of the world to confound the wise; and God hath chosen the weak things of the world to confound the things which are mighty; And base things of the world, and things which are despised, hath God chosen, yea, and things which are not, to bring to nought things that are: That no flesh should glory in his presence.

When God lifts us up, there is no struggle. When God does a thing, it is done well.

When God does the work, it will last. You may not have to take a tiny step at a time until; at last, you reach the top. Get in the Spirit and you will find yourself quickly being lifted to the top. If we are willing to lift up our eyes, God will lift us up. If we are willing to respond to that heavenly pull, He will lift us up. The needs of revival demand it. We often see the limitations, when we should be seeing the miraculous provision of God. All He has to do is send a wind our way and in a moment's time, the necessary changes are taking place. Overnight we go from glory to glory, from one open door to the next.

Not only will we not look to temporal things in the days ahead, we won't even consider them. We will be so consumed with the eternal realm that temporal things will seem as nothing to us. We can no longer afford to live only in the natural realm. We must live in the supernatural. Let yourself soar away and be changed from glory to glory. Receive greater and greater glory, greater and greater revelation, greater and greater insight, greater and greater provision.

Let the hastening of the Spirit be felt down deep in your spirit. We are hastening unto the coming of the Lord, hastening unto the fullness of His purposes. It is through the revelation of the Spirit that you will be elevated. You will no longer move up a step at a time. You will suddenly go from the bottom step to the top step. You will suddenly move up from the lower floors to the upper floors. Don't stand by and watch as others are lifted up. It's also you that the Lord wants to lift up.

God is giving us the opportunity to get ready for revival. Many people feel that they cannot give Him the time needed for revival right now. Their lives are far too complicated and their involvements are too many. God is dealing with us to set our affairs in order so that we will be available for that great and glorious move of God which is coming and in many places, is already here. Lord will lift you up and move you about and you will know that the hand of the Lord is mightily upon you and that all that has happened to you in the past has been to bring you to this day.

God is working on your behalf and has gone before you to prepare the way, so that He can do a glorious thing in you. He has set before you a broad gate. You will not have to squeeze through a narrow opening, for He has opened a broad door of entrance and acceptance for you and you will be able to go in and accomplish all that He has called you to do. I pity those who still believe that God is not speaking to His people today. God hasn't changed and His desire to communicate with His people is just as real today as it has always been. He wants to speak to YOU. His voice will fall upon your spirit as ointment that brings healing to your spirit from every doubt and unbelief of the past. His voice will be a balm for every hurt and every wound so that you can walk forward in confidence and become part of the revival that is coming to God's people. Get ready for revival!

Fan the revival fires in me. Cause me and every circumstance of my life to be ready to be used in revival.

Habakkuk 2:14 For the earth shall be filled with the knowledge of the glory of the LORD, as the waters cover the sea.

We want to see revival in our land more even than we want our necessary food. We declare revival glory from border to border. We must also work to create thirst in others. How do we do that? When people hear God speak, they want to hear Him speak more often. When they feel His touch, they want to feel His touch more often. Once they have experienced new revelation, they want to receive more new revelation. God knows how to make us hungry and He will do it for us if we will let Him.

Each of us has a list of things we don't like. But when we do that, we are only limiting ourselves. We can enjoy eating many things that the ordinary person might not enjoy, or we can limit ourselves to the few things we acquired a taste for while growing up. The choice is ours to make. Nobody can force you to like something or to try it and see if you might develop a taste for it. Many people who are hungry for God are frustrated by not having a church near them which is flowing in revival. It can be a problem, but it is no excuse not to get into what God is doing.

If your church is flowing in the river and the river is flowing in your church, count yourself blessed. Often, this is not the case. Some churches have a fine building, a lovely choir and marvelous programs, but there is no flow of glory in their midst and therefore, little life. If that is the case with the church you attend, it is still no excuse for you to fail to get in the river and let the river flow in you. God responds to hungry hearts. If you are attending a church where the flow of the river is not yet known, I encourage you to start a prayer meeting in your home where you can let God have His way. Make yourself available to God every day. The Lord will teach you and you will know His hand on your shoulders in a new way in the days ahead. He will be so close, whispering in your ear, speaking into your heart, writing on your spirit. You can be among those who are simple, yet profound. You can know the mysteries hidden since the foundation of the world. You can know, not by the understanding of the flesh, but by the revelation of the Spirit. The Lord will lift you into His Spirit again and again until rivers flow in you and through you to bless all those around you.

The touch of revival that is being experienced in various parts of the world is creating a hunger and people are willing to travel for the sake of revival. They want to be in revival meetings and when they travel that far, their expectations are high. The people were ready to move into the things of God, ready to rejoice, ready to dance, ready to pray more energetically and because those who convened the conference wanted to be successful, they were forced to come into a liberty they didn't have before. Revival is coming because of the hunger of the people. In former days, we often saw revival beginning on the platform and moving out to the congregation. Now, however, it seems to be beginning with the people themselves. This is forcing leaders to travel to places where revival is taking place and to get a touch of revival on their lives so that they will have something with which to feed their people. Some pastors, when faced with the changes that revival requires, are still reluctant. They sometimes need several trips to revival sites before they are willing to throw everything to the wind and obey the voice of God.

Traditions and inhibitions don't fall off easily. But if we are genuinely hungry for revival, we will do whatever it takes to achieve it. If you desire it, anything is possible. Some people who have never prophesied before and certainly never over an individual, are prophesying as if they have done it their whole life. Once you get that freedom, it's yours. It may take some a very long time to make up their minds to stand on the end of the diving board and longer still, to take that leap of faith. They may run up to the edge and back again several times, trying to get up their nerve. Once they have made up their minds to take the plunge, however, diving will become second nature to them. You can ride a bicycle if you want, or you can stand back and imagine how very difficult it might be to do such a thing or how easily you could fall and hurt yourself. The choice is yours. You can drive a car, or you can think of all the reasons it would be too difficult and dangerous to learn. Many times our hunger or lack of hunger makes all the difference in this regard. If you are hungry enough for it, you will take the plunge and do whatever is necessary to learn.

When you're not hungry, there is no motivation to even try. When God says something to us, let us respond to Him immediately. Why should we wait? Don't wait for the end of the service. Don't wait for a better opportunity. Get so hungry that you go to the table the first time you are called. If the water is there and the invitation is there and the opportunity is there, what are we waiting for? It is time to swim on out into the river of God.

Ezekiel 47:5 Afterward he measured a thousand; and it was a river that I could not pass over: for the waters were risen, waters to swim in, a river that could not be passed over.

The water that God is calling us to swim in is wonderful, but unless we start swimming, we cannot know how wonderful it is. If there is no swimming, the water cannot be appreciated or utilized. The waters of God are glorious. They are deep enough. They are pure enough. Start swimming. They become "waters to swim in" only if we get in and swim.

Whether we are doing a new stroke or an old stroke, whether we are on our face or our back or our side, we are called to swim. These are days for swimming. Don't even talk about the river unless you are ready to swim in it. If you try to get out into deep waters without being willing to swim in them, you might get yourself in trouble. When the children of Israel came to the Red Sea, it looked to them like an impenetrable barrier. But no sooner had the Egyptians begun to approach them from behind than they got busy crying out to God for the sea to open. Sometimes God has to use the situations of our lives to motivate us to do the right thing. If you have no desire to swim on out in God's water, He may permit something to happen that will give you that desire. This is not the time to harmonize about the river. It is time to get in and start swimming. Some would describe the varying shades of color found in the river; some would speak of its fragrance; and some would concentrate on the fish to be found in it. None of that is wrong, but some people are so wrapped up in the river that they are known as "river people," but still they don't swim.

Get in and start doing a few strokes. Stop picnicking on the banks of the river. Jump in. There are too many people where the things of God have become old and they no longer have a sense of appreciation for them. Some of those who work in the Gospel are the worst offenders. If you talk about God, they think you have taken your work home with you. I enjoy being with those who talk about Him, those who never tire of hearing the same stories of His goodness over and over again. Unless you get hungry and cooperate with God, there isn't much He can do for you.

We don't want to be rushed when we are communing with God. We don't want to be rushed to get up from the floor if we happen to be lying there under the power of God.

In the anointing and in the glory, seeds of greatness are sown into our lives. It happens when we hunger. When God is doing something, how can people be so nonchalant, as if they could not care less? That's not even polite. Let's get out and see what God is doing. Go, drink at the fountain and see how God is doing it.

Each place He does it a little differently because our perceptions are different and our yieldings are different, but it's the same revival; it's the same river; it's the same glory that God is pouring forth. If we are thirsty, there is a simple solution. Come and drink. The three elements are important. Be thirsty; come to Jesus; and drink. When you do these things, rivers of living water are guaranteed to flow forth out of your innermost being. We have no problem understanding these steps when we are baptized in the Holy Spirit. Without a hunger we will not come to Jesus. And once we are there, we must take the step of drinking by faith, receiving what He offers us. And when we do it, a river is released within us. Let God birth within you today a genuine hunger for revival, for He has promised:

Matthew 5:6 Blessed are they which do hunger and thirst after righteousness: for they shall be filled.

2 Peter 1:16-20 For we have not followed cunningly devised fables, when we made known unto you the power and coming of our Lord Jesus Christ, but were eyewitnesses of his majesty. For he received from God the Father honour and glory, when there came such a voice to him from the excellent glory, This is my beloved Son, in whom I am well pleased. And this voice which came from heaven we heard, when we were with him in the holy mount. We have also a more sure word of prophecy; whereunto ye do well that ye take heed, as unto a light that shineth in a dark place, until the day dawn, and the day star arise in your hearts: Knowing this first, that no prophecy of the scripture is of any private interpretation.

If we are willing to respond and move with the Holy Ghost, what God has spoken will come to pass and no one alive can stop it. The secret is our response when we are moved by the Holy Ghost. One of the most wonderful aspects of this current revival is that the Spirit of God is teaching us to respond to Him and nothing could be more important. When God wants to speak, let us be those whom He can use.

Every revival begins with the most unlikely people. It didn't happen as a result of the will of man. You don't initiate it, you just respond to it. When you feel something churning within, when you feel something spinning inside, it is time to act. We will not lean on our own understanding in the days to come.

Prophecy sets in motion a creative force that no man alive can stop. Men can't control what is happening to you and to me. God is sovereign.

Psalms 133:1-3 A Song of degrees of David. Behold, how good and how pleasant it is for brethren to dwell together in unity! It is like the precious ointment upon the head, that ran down upon the beard, even Aaron's beard: that went down to the skirts of his garments; As the dew of Hermon, and as the dew that descended upon the mountains of Zion: for there the LORD commanded the blessing, even life for evermore.

John 17:22 And the glory which thou gavest me I have given them; that they may be one, even as we are one:

The one thing I have learned is that for Revival Glory to come we must be in unity. The number of people can be few but to be unified or on the same page is a must. There are moments when I am sure that glory brings unity and there are other moments when I know that unity brings glory. They are part and partial of each other. God has ordained that we experience the oil of unity. If we are to have the glory of God, we must know the unity of the Spirit among us. The degree of the revelation of the glory will come in proportion to the way we allow God to unite us. This is precisely why the enemy fights unity and harmony in the Body of Christ.

Isaiah 6:4, 5 And the posts of the door moved at the voice of him that cried, and the house was filled with smoke. Then said I, Woe is me! for I am undone; because I am a man of unclean lips, and I dwell in the midst of a people of unclean lips: for mine eyes have seen the King, the LORD of hosts.

We seem capable of seeing only the faults and failures of others. But when the touch of God begins to come to us, when the glory begins to be manifested in our midst, suddenly we recognize that we are the "undone" ones. And it doesn't matter much if we are a little "undone" or if we are a lot "undone." Some people have conquered all the majors, but still have a lot of minors to deal with. Only the glory makes them aware of their lack and then corrects it.

I want to see into realms of glory. I want to see the face of the Lord in every service. I want to see those things which have been prepared for us from the foundation of the world. Just as the oil ran down from the top of Aaron's head down to his beard and on down his garments, to the very skirts, the anointing of glory will cover us completely in these last days as we join hands as brothers and sisters in Christ. It is impossible for us to sit together in heavenly places if we cannot sit together in the flesh, united by the Spirit.

When you purpose for unity, the enemy will throw everything he can in your direction, until you will have despair of ever achieving it.

Romans 12:18 If it be possible, as much as lieth in you, live peaceably with all men.

But God is accepting no excuses in these last days. It is unity or else. I believe that the secret of unity is for each of us to focus our eyes more and more upon Jesus.

The Spirit of God is faithful. He wants us to excel. He wants us to live in the cloud. He wants our houses to be continually "filled with smoke." In fact, He wants our houses to be known more for the continual presence of the smoke than for anything else that people might remember us for. Let people feel the smoke of God's presence when they visit you and they will be moved by it.

We need to stop asking people what denomination they belong to. It doesn't matter. It has nothing to do with revival. I don't care what denomination they belong to and I am convinced that God doesn't care either. It is immaterial. God is bringing forth holy anointing oil that causes brothers to sit together in heavenly places and not to feel the frustrations of one another's limitations. Some people get so agitated just being in the same room together. How can we get God's oil flowing in our lives, if this is our attitude? When the oil of unity is present, it is easy for the house to be "filled with smoke." When the unity is absent, you experience a struggle. God cannot allow His glory to rest in that place. When unity exists, you find things happening easily and quickly. The smoke becomes so strong it is almost like a curtain in front of you, like a thick fog. More and more God is going to bring forth the glory of His presence in our midst. If you covet the smoke, you must also covet the oil, for the two go together unity and glory.

I have seen people robbed of great anointings and great ministries because they refused to deal with their bitter feelings.

God is ready to pour out His glory upon us — if we will properly deal with whatever it is that is hindering us. I find that when I cry out for His help, God is there and always answers and when I do meet a person who has wronged me, I can genuinely embrace that person with Christian love. I know that's not "normal," but God knows how to perform the miracle. If you want to be those who know the house "filled with smoke," be those who experience the flowing of the oil of unity. It doesn't matter if you don't agree totally on doctrinal issues. Enjoy the praises of God together. And when you are all focused on the goodness of the Lord, at that moment there is unity. It is He that unites us, not our doctrinal positions.

Hosea 6:1-3 Come, and let us return unto the LORD: for he hath torn, and he will heal us; he hath smitten, and he will bind us up. After two days will he revive us: in the third day he will raise us up, and we shall live in his sight. Then shall we know, if we follow on to know the LORD: his going forth is prepared as the morning; and he shall come unto us as the rain, as the latter and former rain unto the earth.

I have met many people who are revival specialists. They can tell you the details of every revival that ever took place and why and how it happened. They have read every book available on revival. But many of those people miss revival when it comes. In fact, some of them wouldn't know a revival if it hit them in the face. In every revival, there are certain things that we should expect. For one, we should expect souls to be saved.

Every revival should also experience the healing power of God. Healing doesn't have to dominate our services. We can take a few minutes of each service to minister to the physical needs of the people. It can be done through the word of knowledge, by speaking out the needs God shows you in specific people and declaring their healing. You can do this without calling people to come forward and many can be healed in a short space of time. Healing doesn't have to be the whole service, but in great revival, healing should at least be part of it.

Revival brings us variety. It brings prophecies, miracles, the baptism in the Holy Ghost, deliverance, release from emotional problems, laying hold of the promises of God concerning finances and a wide spectrum of other blessings that God is pouring out in the Earth. In the midst of the glory, some will be called to preach whether at home or out among the nations. All of this should happen in revival glory.

There is broadness to the purposes of God in every service. Let us look for more than one aspect of the Spirit at work in our midst. Revival is a time for miracles and God is telling us that we are moving into the day of creative miracles and that we should all believe Him for it.

God is giving us wonderful signs and wonders to confirm His Word. Stay open to God and what He is doing. It may seem strange to you at first, but eventually you will understand it.

A Church group in Australia bought a bunch of my books. They were so hungry for the Glory of God. They asked for me to release impartation over the books before I sent them. I did and really felt the power of God. After they received them they read all the books and passed them through their Church. I keep receiving emails of the new things they are experiencing. They are now seeing healings, miracles and signs and wonders. The reports are so awesome because God has awakened a new fire in them.

Revival is changing all of us and we are getting more liberty. When people cannot control themselves and helplessly fall down in the power of the Spirit, it encourages them to know that God is real and that what He is doing in them is also real. One of the greatest signs of every revival is the new music that God brings forth. Every great revival produces its own music.

Not everything about revival is pleasant. Every revival is persecuted and often that persecution comes from those who were involved in the previous revival. They think God has to do things in the same way He did it with them and if it is done differently, they imagine that it cannot be from God.

We should expect revival to sweep into many different denominational groups. The Litchfield Revival had many different denominations and even Catholics came through.

Exodus 33:12-15 And Moses said unto the LORD, See, thou sayest unto me, Bring up this people: and thou hast not let me know whom thou wilt send with me. Yet thou hast said, I know thee by name, and thou hast also found grace in my sight. Now therefore, I pray thee, if I have found grace in thy sight, shew me now thy way, that I may know thee, that I may find grace in thy sight: and consider that this nation is thy people. And he said, My presence shall go with thee, and I will give thee rest. And he said unto him, If thy presence go not with me, carry us not up hence.

If God is not with us, we don't want to be there. We might be in the finest gathering with the most exciting people. Thank

God that He is showing forth His presence in this day and hour. God's presence is the glory.

Exodus 33:21, 22 And the LORD said, Behold, there is a place by me, and thou shalt stand upon a rock: And it shall come to pass, while my glory passeth by, that I will put thee in a clift of the rock, and will cover thee with my hand while I pass by:

We're living in a different day. God is not just passing by. He's resting; He's abiding; He is causing us to live in His glory, His holy presence. The Lord loves to be with those who respond to His love, those who love to be in His presence. This doesn't mean that God no longer delights to give miracles. He does. This doesn't mean that God no longer wants to heal. He does. But what we are beginning to learn is that there are miracles in His very presence. There is healing in His very presence. Without

Him having to speak a word, a miracle can take place. His presence performs the miraculous. Without Him having to reach forth His hand and touch anyone, a miracle can take place. His presence produces miracles. There is a glory in God's presence and we are learning to appreciate that manifestation of His presence among us. I don't want to go to church where His presence is not manifested. The worship might be the finest; the sermon might be the greatest; but I would rather be in a place where the worship is not as musically gifted (as far as the world is concerned), but is made up of those who can sing in the glory and can bring the glory into my soul and into my spirit.

GLORY: EXPANDING GOD'S PRESENCE: DISCOVER HOW TO MANIFEST GOD'S GLORY

I love to be with those who gather to be with Him, for when it happens; suddenly His presence is felt tangibly among us.

The glory affects you in tangible ways:

Exodus 34:29 And it came to pass, when Moses came down from mount Sinai with the two tables of testimony in Moses' hand, when he came down from the mount, that Moses wist not that the skin of his face shone while he talked with him.

The shine on the face of Moses was the evidence of the presence of God. You can't be in His presence without it becoming visible in your life. I had always considered that the glory radiating from the face of Moses was a reflection, that because he had been standing face to face with the Lord, the light from the countenance of the Lord had shone onto Moses face and that external experience had worked its way inward. His face shone so brightly that the people were unable to look at him. That's what God wants to do for us in these days.

We formerly thought that only Moses could have had such a great experience, but now we know that we are all destined to see the glory of God and to reflect it to the world. Moses was in God's presence longer than most of us, but as we get into it more and more, spending time with Him, communing with Him, worshiping Him, we will find that the glorious light of the Gospel of Jesus Christ not only shines into our hearts, but shines forth from our lives as well. Many of us are just now beginning to come into the experience that Moses had on the mount with God. It comes when we genuinely hunger for God's presence, when we cry out to Him, "Show me Your glory." Just as Jesus was changed before the eyes of the disciples, we are being changed by the manifestation of the glory of the

Lord. He is changing us from glory to glory. These are revival days in which He is working those transforming graces into our lives and He is doing it by the power of His Spirit. I want to declare, as did Moses: if God's presence goes not with me, I just don't want to go.

I don't want to go where He has not gone before me in the fullness of His glory, in that manifestation of His presence. He is causing the veil to be taken from our eyes, the blinders to fall away, the scales to drop. He is removing the hindrances and the limitations of our own minds and our own thinking and is causing even the crust that has been upon our hearts through the cares of this life to be removed from us, that we might experience His glory in a new and greater way. He is revealing Himself unto us by the power of His Holy Spirit.

The day is upon us that when others look at us, they will see the visible glory of the Lord standing beside us. This is the glory that He desires to manifest in these days, so that some will say, "You didn't come alone." There's nothing like the presence of the Lord. He is with us, not only by promise, but by experience. We can feel Him. The more we live in His presence the more determined we are, like Moses, that if His presence goes not with us, we ourselves will not go. We are determined to stay in the glory.

We must allow God to lift us often into those realms by His Spirit. When most people speak about the Lord being an All-Consuming Fire, they usually say it in reference to sins in their lives they are sure they need to repent of. While it's true that many of us have extra baggage we need to get rid of, those of us who are earnestly seeking God are living a sinless

GLORY: EXPANDING GOD'S PRESENCE:
DISCOVER HOW TO MANIFEST GOD'S GLORY

life. When we do make a mistake, the Holy Spirit is quick to convict us and we quickly ask for forgiveness and go on.

Exodus 40:36, 37 And when the cloud was taken up from over the tabernacle, the children of Israel went onward in all their journeys: But if the cloud were not taken up, then they journeyed not till the day that it was taken up.

Numbers 9:17-23 And when the cloud was taken up from the tabernacle, then after that the children of Israel journeyed: and in the place where the cloud abode, there the children of Israel pitched their tents. At the commandment of the LORD the children of Israel journeyed, and at the commandment of the LORD they pitched: as long as the cloud abode upon the tabernacle they rested in their tents. And when the cloud tarried long upon the tabernacle many days, then the children of Israel kept the charge of the LORD, and journeyed not. And so it was, when the cloud was a few days upon the tabernacle; according to the commandment of the LORD they abode in their tents, and according to the commandment of the LORD they journeyed. And so it was, when the cloud abode from even unto the morning, and that the cloud was taken up in the morning, then they journeyed: whether it was by day or by night that the cloud was taken up, they journeyed. Or whether it were two days, or a month, or a year, that the cloud tarried upon the tabernacle, remaining thereon, the children of Israel abode in their tents, and journeyed not: but when it was taken up, they journeyed. At the commandment of the LORD they rested in the tents, and at the commandment of the LORD they journeyed: they kept the charge of the LORD, at the commandment of the LORD by the hand of Moses.

In the Bible days the cloud was the visible sign of God's presence, just as glory is the manifested presence of God with us today. Sometimes they saw the cloud and sometimes they didn't and glory can be visible or invisible. It comes by revelation. The cloud was a tangible sign of change, just as the glory cloud is for us. The cloud was equivalent to the spoken commandment of the Lord, a visible sign of the spoken Word of God. The people, I'm sure, often could not understand just why they should move on. They were so obviously in the will of God at the right place, at the right time and in the right circumstances. Why were they now being left without a cloud? And there are people all over America and around the world today who are sitting where they have been sitting for many years. They believe they are sitting under the cloud and don't even realize that the cloud has moved on. They got absorbed in the place where the cloud dwelt in former times and didn't see it lifting and moving on. Many lovely Christians find themselves sitting in a beautiful tabernacle that once knew the glory, once knew the presence of God and once knew His revelation.

They are now in dismay, wondering why they are not feeling the glory as before. If they had only been looking up, they might have seen the glory moving on. But they were too wrapped up in their surroundings to discern that God was doing a new thing. Some people may stay where they are now for a very long time, for they have enough material to sustain them as they were. They can continue, as if the cloud was present, but they are only deceiving themselves. The cloud has moved on. Trying to do anything without God's presence is what Paul meant when he wrote to the Corinthians:

GLORY: EXPANDING GOD'S PRESENCE: DISCOVER HOW TO MANIFEST GOD'S GLORY

1 Corinthians 13:1 Though I speak with the tongues of men and of angels, and have not charity, I am become as sounding brass, or a tinkling cymbal.

The ability to draw a crowd is not an indication that someone is living under the cloud of God's glory. We must learn to sense the moving of the cloud and learn to sense the glory upon a person. We cannot afford to stick with someone just because of a former greatness. It is time to move on. Move with the cloud. Old revelation does not inspire the soul to greatness.

Old revelation does not move us to excellence. Old revelation has the effect of putting us to sleep. We don't want to live any longer in old revelation. Move on if you want to live under the cloud, for it is moving. We all repeat wonderful old stories. We all tell things that God did for us in the past. That's okay, but if, in the midst of the telling, God doesn't speak something new into our spirits for that particular day and that particular service, we are missing out on what He is doing in this day. I, for one, am not satisfied to know that I have developed the ability to soak in the presence of God in a way that few have. I am not satisfied with the strength of the stakes I have driven into the surrounding soil. I am satisfied only with the glory and if the glory moves on, I must move with it, or my soul will not be satisfied and at peace. Yes, I believe in stability and I want you to stay where you are just as long as God wants you there. But be careful. Don't let the glory cloud move on without you. Moving is not always easy. It involves pulling up stakes, packing things up and lightening the load. But whatever you must do to rise up and follow the cloud of glory that is moving on, do it.

The wheel within the wheel is turning. Don't miss what God is doing because of something upon which you have set your affections. Hold lightly the things of this world and be ready to move on with the cloud at a moment's notice. If you feel the fire within the fire burning, don't hesitate. Don't turn aside for anything of this world. Move on. If you sense the glory rising, you must rise with it. If you sense the cloud moving on, you must move on with it. It doesn't matter if you just got your stakes down like you wanted them. The move of God doesn't happen according to your timing. God cannot always accommodate your schedule. He moves sovereignly, as He wills and if you don't move with Him, you will be left behind. Learn to live under the cloud and not let anything cause you to come out from under it. Let it be under you and over you, so that you are encased in it, enveloped by it and consumed by it. Be clothed with the glory cloud of God's Spirit.

The cloud is so all-consuming that in the days ahead we will see ministries that have resisted certain aspects of the move of God's Spirit in the past now being baptized in the cloud and doing things they never imagined themselves doing. Lord, hasten the day. Oh, move with the cloud. It may seem to some like a hard statement to say that some churches don't know that the glory cloud is no longer with them. Whether He moves on and we stay put, or we move on and He stays put, either way we're in trouble. We can't live without Him. May God make us to realize when it happens so that we can turn back to find Him. Some people are never available when God wants to move on. If they don't have something "really important" to do first, they will think of something "really important" to do. So they miss God's best for their lives every time. God

GLORY: EXPANDING GOD'S PRESENCE:
DISCOVER HOW TO MANIFEST GOD'S GLORY

is tired of waiting on some people. If you have that spirit of always wanting things to happen in your time, you need to shake yourself and get up and run after God's glory. There is too much to lose. Get over your willfulness. It's not going to happen in your way and in your time. God is Good and when His chariot is moving on, you must move with it.

You may feel like you just got things planned as you wanted them, that you were finally able to put some finishing touches on your dwelling place and to decorate it as you have wanted to for so long, only to see the cloud lifting and beginning to move away. This is a painful experience for many. Just when they think they have gotten their life under control, God is moving again and things are changing. If you are one of those people, what can you do? You have no alternative. You must follow the cloud. Give up what you have to give up; give away what you have to give away; sell what you have to sell; but move on with the glory cloud. Don't let anything or anybody hold you back. There is no other alternative. I did this at the end of the two year long Revival in Litchfield, IL. There were many rumors and even lies of why I left. I left and it was for the Glory of the Lord. Even the ones closest to you may be pushing God's Glory away. You have to come to a decision it's either them or God's Glory Cloud. If the presence of God is not with you in what you are doing, turn back to find Him.

If His presence has gone on ahead and you have not realized it, rise up and go quickly after Him. Don't delay. If you have been sidetracked by trying a particular method that has borne fruit for someone else, turn back to find the Lord's presence. He is more important than a method, a system, or a program. Come back to the simplicity of His presence. Under the cloud is the only place of safety. It is the only place of divine health. It is the only place of guaranteed provision. It is the only place of sure revelation. It is the only place which guarantees us salvation for our households and for our nation. When the glory cloud began to move, the people of Israel had to quickly pack up their belongings, often, no doubt, having to lighten the load, so that they could move on. Whatever it takes, that's what we want to do. When God poured His Spirit upon the disciples in the Upper Room, in just a few days time the structure of the spiritual movement was totally changed and God had raised up an entirely new group of leaders, those who trusted the Spirit of God.

If people have become static, if they are exactly where they have been for some time, if they haven't changed in ten years, I would consider them in danger of being passed over. God is moving on.

Revival is spontaneous and we must learn to be spontaneous. Sometimes we need to stop every other activity and listen carefully to what the Spirit is saying. We can get so busy that we don't even notice that we are being left behind. Stop every other activity and become sensitive to the glory cloud. Then, when it starts to move, rise up and go quickly after it. Some people are distressed about any kind of change, but that's foolish. God has given us His Word and we know the intents of His heart. He has but one desire for us and that one desire is that we be changed from glory to glory. He has never moved a person to a lesser glory than they've already experienced. Change, therefore, is our friend. The changes God is sending into our lives are intended to work in us "a far more exceeding and eternal weight of glory." In fact, change becomes the measure of the glory.

It doesn't take long to get ready once one is convinced that moving is the right thing to do. It's the decisions that take a long time. The moving itself doesn't take very long. Getting in the frame of mind necessary for moving is much more difficult than the moving process itself. Put aside every excuse and begin to move with the cloud of God's glory. We like to make our own decisions, but it is easier and safer for us to let God make them. When God shows you that it is moving time, it may not seem like a convenient day or a convenient time. God is nudging us to get into the fullness of the flow of the river of God. The more you touch the heavenly, the more you know the glory realm, the more you want to know it, reaching in beyond anything that we have known or experienced. If we are willing, God will help us make a quicker shift from the old to the new. There is a transition period in which we have a mixture of old and new. Sometimes we have more of the old than the new and other times more of the new than the old.

But God is helping us to flow into those greater realms of His glory, not just having spurts of it, touches of it and glimpses of it, but rivers of it. Let us be lifted up into realms of glory that we have never before experienced. I will not be satisfied with anything less and I know you won't either. There is a rhythm to the glory and when we speak of the glory cloud we speak of moving. Even when the glory cloud remained still, those who were under it were moving. They were moving from one realm to another realm, from one dimension to another dimension, from one authority to another authority and from one glory to another glory. We must learn to sit under the glory cloud and when that glory cloud begins to move, we must rise up and move on with it. All of those who are sensing the cloud of glory in their lives are also experiencing a sense of acceleration in the movement of events around them. Historically, the cloud moved only every few decades or every few years and the people of God sensed a change in what He was doing. Today, however, we are experiencing many sudden and unexpected changes.

Sometimes we settle one night thinking that we have settled down for a while. But no sooner have we settled in than the cloud lifts and begins to move on. If we are not to be left behind, we must quickly strike our tents and rush to keep up with the moving cloud. The cloud never goes backward. When God lifts us into a new realm of glory, He has shown us that it is important never to go back to the former realm. Move in the cloud and move with the cloud. Get to know the movings of the Spirit, with the cloud over you, with the cloud under you, with the cloud surrounding you. When you are moving with the cloud, you have nothing to worry about.

Revelations 4:1, 2 After this I looked, and, behold, a door was opened in heaven: and the first voice which I heard was as it were of a trumpet talking with me; which said, Come up hither, and I will shew thee things which must be hereafter. And immediately I was in the spirit: and, behold, a throne was set in heaven, and one sat on the throne.

Ezekiel had a similar experience. He said:

Ezekiel 37:1 The hand of the LORD was upon me, and carried me out in the spirit of the LORD, and set me down in the midst of the valley which was full of bones,

GLORY: EXPANDING GOD'S PRESENCE: DISCOVER HOW TO MANIFEST GOD'S GLORY

This carrying away is wonderful because God Himself chooses the itinerary. When we choose, we can sometimes be disappointed, but when God chooses, we are never disappointed. He is sovereign God and when He carries us away, we're not sure where we are going. John was taken directly to the throne and began to see it in all its glory. He saw what was in front of it, what was behind it and what was around it. God may carry you to some other place and there show you His purposes to drop faith into your heart to believe for the greater thing, to teach you in realms that you have never known. God does not want us to be earthbound.

We were not designed for this world and when we are caught up in the Spirit, He lets us know, in a way that we could not know otherwise, that we are only pilgrims here on this Earth, that we are not natural, but spiritual. In the moments when the glory is manifested, ordinary people like you and I are suddenly carried away and permitted to see things that are not visible to the physical eye. Just as there is natural seeing, there is spiritual seeing. Some people are teaching us that we should picture what we want God to do and believe Him for it, but I prefer to let God choose for me. I let Him give me the vision, rather than me trying to give Him the vision. I could never imagine things as glorious as He shows me. I could never even begin to dream of all that is in the heart of God for me. My own expectations are so small in comparison to His expectations for me. Get your head into the river. Let the river touch your hearing; let it touch your seeing; let it touch your reasoning faculties; let it touch every part of your life. There has never been a day of revelation like this day.

Ordinary people are seeing things that only great people knew of in days gone by:

Matthew 13:17 For verily I say unto you, That many prophets and righteous men have desired to see those things which ye see, and have not seen them; and to hear those things which ye hear, and have not heard them.

Psalms 8:2 Out of the mouth of babes and sucklings hast thou ordained strength because of thine enemies, that thou mightest still the enemy and the avenger.

In order to be carried away in the glory, you must first learn to yield yourself to the Spirit. The Apostle Paul wrote:

Romans 6:13 Neither yield ye your members as instruments of unrighteousness unto sin: but yield yourselves unto God, as those that are alive from the dead, and your members as instruments of righteousness unto God.

It's all in the yielding. You can get into the river just as quickly as you want to. You can get into the glory just as quickly as you want to.

If you are hungry enough, you'll yield. Paul continued:

Romans 6:19 I speak after the manner of men because of the infirmity of your flesh: for as ye have yielded your members servants to uncleanness and to iniquity unto iniquity; even so now yield your members servants to righteousness unto holiness.

Philippians 4:19 But my God shall supply all your need according to his riches in glory by Christ Jesus.

When we become a praising people, a people of the glory cloud, we will find our needs automatically supplied. I don't want to know the throne of God only as a place of petition. We can become totally consumed with problems, sickness, financial want, emotional problems, etc., and miss the great things God wants to do for us. Our God is great and we must not spend all our time concerned for physical and material needs.

There is provision in the cloud of God's glory just as the natural cloud gives provision for the earth:

Isaiah 55:10 For as the rain cometh down, and the snow from heaven, and returneth not thither, but watereth the earth, and maketh it bring forth and bud, that it may give seed to the sower, and bread to the eater:

Stop looking at the things that are seen. Stop going over and over your budget, trying to figure out how it's all going to be possible. That's an act of unbelief. There are some things that you don't want to examine too closely. Just get the overall picture. You don't need to be frightened by the details. Keep your eyes on the Heavenlies. See the eternal, the invisible, things of God. Some fail to move with the glory cloud because they think that a cloud has no substance and that there is nothing practical in it. How foolish! We don't need anything more substantial than the cloud of God's glory. That's as substantial as you can get. If you have nothing else, you can leave home based on the moving of the cloud.

Matthew 19:29 And every one that hath forsaken houses, or brethren, or sisters, or father, or mother, or wife, or children, or lands, for my name's sake, shall receive an hundredfold, and shall inherit everlasting life.

You have nothing to fear when you are following the cloud of God's glory. That cloud is so substantial that it can cause you to leave every other security behind and you will know that it is enough. As long as you are conscious that the cloud is over your head and as long as you are willing to rise up when it begins to move and to hold still when it stops, you have nothing to worry about financially. God will do for you the things He has appointed. You don't need to have resources in order for God to use you these days. Just get under His cloud and He will take care of the rest. You don't need to be famous in order to be used by God. You just need to get under His glory cloud. He can put you at the forefront of situations, just as easily as He can put another person there and He can provide for your needs just as easily as He can provide for another.

If God has opened a door for you in the Spirit, you don't need any other open door. His glory is sufficient. If you insist on having something "more substantial," you will miss the will of God for your life. Stop asking God for something "more substantial" and start asking Him to make you sensitive to the cloud of His glory. Ask Him to let you see it and feel it and move with it. Ask Him to teach you when the glory is present and when it is not. Ask Him to make you more alert to the changes of the moment.

I talked about many supernatural provisions in my book The Supernatural Realm. God provided and even multiplied money and still does it in our family today.

You never lose financially by moving with the cloud and resting under it. We have absolutely nothing to fear in the realm of provision when we get into the cloud of God's glory.

Numbers 10:28, 29 Thus were the journeyings of the children of Israel according to their armies, when they set forward. And Moses said unto Hobab, the son of Raguel the Midianite, Moses' father in law, We are journeying unto the place of which the LORD said, I will give it you: come thou with us, and we will do thee good: for the LORD hath spoken good concerning Israel.

Numbers 10:33-36 And they departed from the mount of the LORD three days' journey: and the ark of the covenant of the LORD went before them in the three days' journey, to search out a resting place for them. And the cloud of the LORD was upon them by day, when they went out of the camp. And it came to pass, when the ark set forward, that Moses said, Rise up, LORD, and let thine enemies be scattered; and let them that hate thee flee before thee. And when it rested, he said, Return, O LORD, unto the many thousands of Israel.

I am convinced that God wants to bring us into a realm of glory where we know His rest. He wants all the struggle and striving within us to fall away. He has a place of rest for us, a place of confidence and it is to be found in His glory. We could never find this resting place on our own, but God goes before us and searches out this place of rest. Then we can sit beside His river and rest, knowing that He will supply our every need. We may come into the sanctuary with the distresses of life upon us, but within a few moments spent in God's glory, we are rested.

Ephesians 4:30 And grieve not the holy Spirit of God, whereby ye are sealed unto the day of redemption.

1 Thessalonians 5:19 Quench not the Spirit.

Criticism, bitterness, backbiting and strife will eat up the very harvest you are believing for. One touch of God's glory melts the hardest heart.

Over a period of time I have learned that some of the things which most adversely affect the flow of the glory of God in our midst are these:

- Our desire to please people

- Our fear of appearing too simple, too unlearned
- Our desire to impress people with our education, skills and abilities and with who we are
- Our inability to unlearn what we have already learned when God is attempting to lead us into new things
- Our inability or unwillingness to lay aside tradition
- Our unwillingness to forgive others

God wants to give us all a greater sensitivity in this regard. If we can learn to know the cloud whether there are ten people present or a hundred or five hundred or five thousand or fifty thousand we will be able to stand under the cloud and minister directly from the glory unto the people. This is revival glory. We may have to throw out some of the old in order to obtain the new, but the Lord will help us and teach us. He has promised to be our Instructor.

He has promised to lead us forth and He will, if we are determined to stand under the glory cloud or to stand in it. When you discover things that seem to contribute to the glory, do those things more; and when you find things that seem to diminish the glory, stop doing them. It's as simple as that.

Zechariah 4:6 Then he answered and spake unto me, saying, This is the word of the LORD unto Zerubbabel, saying, Not by might, nor by power, but by my spirit, saith the LORD of hosts.

God wants to do for us. We just get too complicated. The simplicity of a thing is important. This is the reason God has to continually raise up new movements. When the former movement gets so sophisticated and polished that it loses its ability to move out into the flow of new things that God is doing, He is forced to move on. It is possible to get too

GLORY: EXPANDING GOD'S PRESENCE:
DISCOVER HOW TO MANIFEST GOD'S GLORY

organized. Anytime we get to the place that our dependence on the Holy Ghost is limited, He goes elsewhere. In many circles, people can preach whether the Holy Spirit is present or not and most of the time, they do.

When the message is finished, we can all say, "What a great sermon," but few of us can say, "What great glory! What a fresh touch of the Spirit upon the people!"

John 7:38, 39 He that believeth on me, as the scripture hath said, out of his belly shall flow rivers of living water. (But this spake he of the Spirit, which they that believe on him should receive: for the Holy Ghost was not yet given; because that Jesus was not yet glorified.)

Learn to relax in God's presence so that you can be carried by the flow of His River. You can't release the flow; only He can, so let Him do it. Let Him bring you forth into an ease. You can't carry His River, but His River can carry you. Be carried away by the Spirit again and again. Let Him bring you forth into the fullness of this new day. He will do it for you if you will just yield to Him.

As the river flows, revelation flows. As the river flows, vision flows. As the river flows, miracles flow. As the river flows, there is healing and deliverance and victory.

When we begin to flow with the river, we may have no idea where that flow is taking us. If we need to know, the Lord will tell us, but usually we don't need to know. Just get with the flow and as you flow, God will drop the vision into your spirit and prepare you for where the river is taking you. It will sometimes be to an individual, other times to a church or congregation or perhaps to a city, state, or nation. He may even carry you out into the realms of the Heavenlies. Sometimes in order to get into the flow of the glory you must forget your prayer list. Don't worry about it. God will put His thoughts into your spirit. He will bring to your remembrance the things you need to speak with Him about and if He doesn't remind you of something, you had best forget it. He knows what is important at the moment. Let all the dams be removed. Let the river do what it was designed to do. Remove any obstacle to its flow. Most of us would never think of consciously quenching the Spirit; but, at the same time, most of us are not willing to let the river flow. Stop quenching it. Stop preventing it. Stop avoiding it. Let it flow. Stop frustrating God's purposes.

He wants to flood your soul with blessing. Why do we not trust Him? His river has one purpose and that is to give life. Ezekiel declared it:

Ezekiel 47:9 And it shall come to pass, that every thing that liveth, which moveth, whithersoever the rivers shall come, shall live: and there shall be a very great multitude of fish, because these waters shall come thither: for they shall be healed; and every thing shall live whither the river cometh.

Revelations 22:17 And the Spirit and the bride say, Come. And let him that heareth say, Come. And let him that is athirst come. And whosoever will, let him take the water of life freely.

Wherever this river goes, nothing can stay dead. Everything in its path receives life. And the more we allow the river of God to flow through us the less of death will be found in us.

We need to draw on the heavenly dimension and let it flow into us and then flow out of us. That's the key word of the revival. It doesn't matter how great the river is.

If you don't let it flow, its waters become dead and all blessing ceases. You need a river of life and it must be allowed to flow. In connection with flow, there is another word that we must learn and be aware of. It is the word Spontaneous. God is calling us to allow Him to work spontaneously in our midst. When we first get started in the prophetic realm, the exercise of the supernatural gifts of God, He often permits certain things. Later, He will not permit those same things and it is because the giftings of God must be spontaneous.

Flowing is individual and flowing together is congregational. This is the reason praise and worship is being restored in the congregation. Many of the things that are happening to us as congregations used to happen to us as we worshiped alone in our homes. That's why we should do many things together. We should stand together; we should lift up our voices together; we should raise our hands together and we should dance together.

At first, it may be a mechanical lifting up, but as we obey the Lord in this act of unity, before long we will feel the moving of the river of God and know that we are one in Him. We may begin worshiping as many voices, but when He does the miracle in us, those many voices become one voice. As we join together at the feet of Jesus, we must each lay aside our individual agenda, so that we can all find His agenda and begin to flow together to the goodness of the Lord. The glory of God is only revealed in its fullness when we are together.

There were so many times in Litchfield, IL that we would call a time of worship and every one of our core group would come and worship together. Some ask how can Revival continue over two years and one answer is we came together and flowed together in unity.

Isaiah 58:14 Then shalt thou delight thyself in the LORD; and I will cause thee to ride upon the high places of the earth, and feed thee with the heritage of Jacob thy father: for the mouth of the LORD hath spoken it.

The joy of the Lord that is coming forth in revival is so important that we must ask God to help us not to attempt to analyze it, but just to enjoy it. If you have never experienced the joy of the Lord, it's time to have that experience. If you have never received holy laughter, it's time for you to receive. You may want to continue to do things in the way you have always done them, but God is saying that it's time for a new way. Get into the flow of the river so that God can cause rivers of living water to flow out of your innermost being to others. Joy is one of the ways God strengthens us. He has chosen it as His strengthening measure. I'm not sure why, you and I might do it differently, but that is God's choice. Joy brings strength:

Nehemiah 8:10 Then he said unto them, Go your way, eat the fat, and drink the sweet, and send portions unto them for whom nothing is prepared: for this day is holy unto our Lord: neither be ye sorry; for the joy of the LORD is your strength.

The joy of the Lord is your strength and the joy of the Lord is my strength. God has placed this strengthening agent into our lives so that we will have sufficient strength for the great gathering, the harvest that God is calling us to bring in - in this last day. We must let God do it in His own way. Some people have to be knocked to the floor the first time they laugh in the Spirit. They can't seem to do it any other way. God can give

GLORY: EXPANDING GOD'S PRESENCE: DISCOVER HOW TO MANIFEST GOD'S GLORY

them the spirit of laughter without having to knock them to the floor. When they feel that spirit coming upon them, they just yield to it and move on out into the flow. If you have to be knocked out in order to do some of these things, then get knocked out often enough so that it becomes easier and easier.

In this realm of glory, greater and greater miracles will take place. God is bringing great transformation to the hearts of people and He is also touching their bodies and taking care of their emotional needs. Some people have criticized the laughing revival because of the fact that some continue to laugh during the course of the sermon.

That, many consider, is irreverent. But, if we stop and consider it, there was obviously something very strange going on at the house of Cornelius while Peter was preaching there.

The Scriptures declare:

Acts 10:44-46 While Peter yet spake these words, the Holy Ghost fell on all them which heard the word. And they of the circumcision which believed were astonished, as many as came with Peter, because that on the Gentiles also was poured out the gift of the Holy Ghost. For they heard them speak with tongues, and magnify God. Then answered Peter,

2 Corinthians 4:17, 18 For our light affliction, which is but for a moment, worketh for us a far more exceeding and eternal weight of glory; While we look not at the things which are seen, but at the things which are not seen: for the things which are seen are temporal; but the things which are not seen are eternal.

I encourage people to see the eternal, but each one must purpose to see, must have a desire to see and be hungry to see.

And each one must believe to see and start reaching out to see. You can't see without making the effort to look. He can only give us a flow of revelation through people who have moved into the revelatory realm and desire to be used of God in this way. I believe some of our best meetings have been when those who have just begun to move into the revelatory realm began to describe what they were seeing. It isn't always easy to describe eternal things with our limited vocabularies, but God will help us to do it. We must speak out what He is showing us, proclaiming and declaring it. It is the "now vision." He is causing us to see Him and we simply must reach out for this revelation. If He doesn't fill our vision more and more, we won't be able to make it in the days to come. He must become all-consuming in our visions. God delights in removing the veil from our eyes and causing every scale to come off, so that we can see and see clearly His glory, the glory of His countenance. Then we will know the glory of His purposes, we will know the glory of His plan and we will walk in realms of glory.

God wants us to live in the realm of vision and we must do it in the days ahead, for it is the revelation of God that will quicken our spirits. There are still many people who don't believe in vision, but that doesn't negate what God is doing. Despite the doubts of many, God is bringing forth the ministry of the seers, those who prophesy by vision. The entire future of our ministries is dependent upon our ability to see into the heavenly realm, therefore God wants to elevate us into a seeing dimension. He wants to cover us with eyes. The anointing to see will cause you to stand in high places. Let there come to you right now eagerness, a sensitivity in the realm of the Spirit. May the anointing for seeing be released in you from this day forward? Seeing into the needs of the people will change the way you preach. We must move from the informational type of preaching that comes from our accumulated wisdom and knowledge into a revelatory preaching that comes to us at the moment. We must be as the prophet of old who opened for the first time a scroll that he had never read and began to declare its contents.

Each of us must reach up, take the scroll and unroll it before the people. It will be fresh bread for all those who hear it. Forget what the former strong points of your ministry have been and start declaring the new things God gives you. Lay aside those former strong points and let your ministry be known for the strength of revelation that will come forth from it in the days ahead. Some of you will begin to have a flow of visions and revelations as you are doing your daily tasks. You don't have to wait until you are in church to receive revelation. What God is showing us sometimes seems to be so simple that we wonder if we dare share it with anyone else. Simple things are often profound. Don't be afraid to share what God is telling you. It will bless someone. God wants to reveal things to you as you walk. God wants to reveal to you the hearts of men. Some people get frightened as they feel an unusual fluttering in their hearts. That's nothing to be worried about. The Holy Spirit is causing an eternal flutter, a quickening of the Spirit. He is teaching you. God is leaning down to whisper secrets in your ear, first one and then the other.

Take hold of what He is saying to you. Take hold of that to which He has called you. Take hold of the ministry to which He has ordained you. Take hold of the city in which He sees fit to establish you. Take hold in the realm of the Spirit. These are days of seeing and possessing what we see. Because God is anointing us more and more to look into the unseen realm, look for the eternal in every service. Look for the glory. Look for the manifestation of it. Let God anoint you unto the excellence of this new day. Because we know it is available, it becomes our responsibility in every service to move into the realms of revelation so that we can bless others with the glory of God. God wants us to go from revealed glory to revealed glory.

Luke 17:20-24 And when he was demanded of the Pharisees, when the kingdom of God should come, he answered them and said, The kingdom of God cometh not with observation: Neither shall they say, Lo here! or, lo there! for, behold, the kingdom of God is within you. And he said unto the disciples, The days will come, when ye shall desire to see one of the days of the Son of man, and ye shall not see it. And they shall say to you, See here; or, see there: go not after them, nor follow them. For as the lightning, that lighteneth out of the one part under heaven, shineth unto the other part under heaven; so shall also the Son of man be in his day.

We must have the eyes of our spirit sensitized more and more so that we can lay hold of the revelations of God as they come forth. This great revival is bringing forth great revelation. It is coming as we sit in the cloud of God's glory. I love revelatory services, in which, one after another, we all prophesy by revelation and by vision. If you want great revelation, you have to believe for it. Then, make yourself available and watch what God will do. Revelation will bring you the understanding of where to go from here, what steps to take next and how to handle the current situation. This is not a onetime experience. God wants to reveal Himself to you every day, in progressions.

GLORY: EXPANDING GOD'S PRESENCE: DISCOVER HOW TO MANIFEST GOD'S GLORY

The nature of revelation is "precept upon precept, line upon line, here a little and there a little."

It's very much like placing the blocks in a building. Piece by piece, it takes form, until, one day, we will have the completed revelation.

We shouldn't get up too quickly from the altar or from falling under the power of God. If you have no reason to get up quickly, linger for a while. Give God the opportunity to reveal Himself to you. If you have tried it and nothing seemingly happened, keep on trying until it does. This is one revelation you simply can't miss. What we see in the Spirit is often like peripheral vision. We can see clearly what is directly ahead of us. Many things, however, pass by on to the side and we don't perceive them very clearly. I see visions while I am preaching and while I am praying for people. I might be looking at the people and focusing on them, but God is giving me something else to see in my peripheral vision. I learned to give attention to it and to focus on it, while focusing on the people. Become sensitive to His desires.

When someone in charge of a service begins to flow in vision, reach out in the Spirit so that you can flow with them. Just as we worship as one voice and we reach out together for prophetic messages and could sometimes tell the next words or phrases of a prophetic message even before they are spoken by another person, likewise we can flow together in vision. We can see the same thing at the same time.

When you see the fire of God, don't immediately think of the fires of persecution. Let God's flames begin to consume you with Himself, with His presence and with His glory. Fire is one of the manifestations of the glory of God and we're going to see it more and more, so get used to it and stop associating it with things that should be burned up and destroyed. As He has done in the past, God is giving His people dreams and visions through this revival. These dreams and visions are not just nice possibilities. We should expect the fulfillment of every single one of them. Another thing that we should expect more of in this revival is to see the angels of God.

Every great revival has experienced such angelic activity and we should expect to see it more in the coming days. You can experience both types of revelation. One is sovereign and the other comes through seeking and searching for God. If you really want the great things of God in your soul, you must be one who longs to know the Lord in a greater way. We must ask. We must look. We must knock. We must ponder. We must let God reveal the answer to us. God's showing us, by His Spirit, the ease in which He's bringing forth revival in this last day and hour. We can have entire weeks of glory, when many move into new realms of the Spirit of God and let His river flow. I'm not disturbed when we don't have preaching in a service. I'd be very happy for one person to start prophesying and flow into the next. God is doing things differently and if we are willing to move with His flow, we don't have to return to old patterns. We can move into new patterns by the revelation of the Spirit of the Living God. God might interrupt some of your plans and He just might turn your plans upside down. We can know by the Spirit of the Lord.

Can we trust the Holy Spirit? Absolutely, we can trust Him. Those who ignore visions are only robbing themselves. And if you have ever given a gift that was not appreciated, you probably didn't try as hard to please that person the next time

GLORY: EXPANDING GOD'S PRESENCE: DISCOVER HOW TO MANIFEST GOD'S GLORY

around. If you want the revelation of the Spirit flowing in your life, appreciate what God's saying to you, even when you don't understand it all. God is not just giving us little things to stir us, to tickle our ears or to make us feel happy. He is showing us great things, eternal things, in the Spirit, things that have the potential to change the course of history in many nations for His glory.

God wants us to be a people of the revelation of the Holy Spirit. Vision is one of the most important methods God is using to reveal Himself to the Church today. Many people have a problem with vision because it generally happens so quickly and passes. We would prefer that it be like a movie that lasts much longer, that it contain much more detail and that we be given much more time to ponder it. But, whether it happens that way or not, don't ever take vision for granted.

Don't ever take the audible voice of God in your spirit for granted. Don't ever become nonchalant about the dreams He gives you in the night season. Some people can say, "I can have a vision any time I want." Well, those people are blessed and they should consider the preciousness of their gift. It is to be treasured. Some people have the ability to make large sums of money. They should appreciate that fact because other people have to make a great effort just to pay their bills on time. When God gives you some greater ability, don't ever take it for granted. Appreciate it. Too many people who have received great abilities in the realm of the Spirit have done less with those abilities than those who have received little. Sometimes when we have only a little ability we appreciate it more and use it more. I don't see as many visions as some, but I talk about every one I get. I get excited about them and reach out to understand what God is showing me and apply it.

Once we had learned that secret, we continued to live by revelation. We can pray, "God, reveal what we need to know about this subject by your Spirit. Reveal what we need to know about this situation by Your Spirit." When we were children, we moved often and unlike those who move on a whim, my parents were always praying to know where the Lord wanted us to move. We moved only by revelations. We never once moved based on what we could afford. We never once moved based on seeing a house the family liked and wanted to live in. Unless God showed us when and where, we didn't move. No wonder we have been so blessed! God didn't give all the revelations to me directly, but I became good at listening to the revelations everyone else was having and many times they were for my instruction as well. Be humble enough to receive from others. Some will only receive from certain individuals, but they limit themselves in this way. Recognize the voice of God, even if he uses a donkey to speak to you. Whenever God has quickened something to my spirit, I have been off and running with it.

There are certain things that God sovereignly shows you, without your having to ponder them. After I had that revelation of the moments dropping down, I lived in that revelation all that day. It was such an amazing, sovereign thing that God had done, without my having pondered them at all. There are other times when we begin a spiritual search concerning something of God, something you're interested in, something you're moving toward, something you want God to reveal to you.

GLORY: EXPANDING GOD'S PRESENCE: DISCOVER HOW TO MANIFEST GOD'S GLORY

God wants us to have tenacity of spirit in seeking Him. He wants us to search out these wonderful things until we are satisfied. It's wonderful when you're in the Spirit and what you know is not by the understanding of the flesh. It's exciting to be on the cutting edge of what God is doing, to know that you're not trained in that way in the natural, but that God has just put you in the middle of it in the Spirit. God will put us in the middle of things for which we have no natural background. We want to know the Lord according to revelation rather than according to our human understanding.

We want to know the Holy of Holies, not architecturally speaking, but according to experience.

If God gives you a jewel that no one else appreciates please don't throw it away. Many Americans have little appreciation for the unfamiliar gems. How many Americans have ever seen a yellow diamond? How many Americans have ever seen a green diamond? Unless you go to the Smithsonian Institute, you may never see these things. That doesn't nullify the fact that they are more rare and therefore, more costly than the more common blue diamonds. The fact that most people, if given the choice, would pick the type of diamond they are most accustomed to seeing, doesn't cancel out the worth of the other. Determine in your heart to search out the deeper things of God. He desires to have a people that sits and ponders.

Luke 2:19 But Mary kept all these things, and pondered them in her heart.

In earlier days of revival, people were much more dependent on the Holy Spirit for revelation.

Daniel 11:32 And such as do wickedly against the covenant shall he corrupt by flatteries: but the people that do know their God shall be strong, and do exploits.

Luke 24:31 And their eyes were opened, and they knew him; and he vanished out of their sight.

We are seeing great miracles performed in the glory, but this revival is not just for the miraculous. The ultimate revival is the revelation of Jesus Christ. You might say, "I already know Him." You may know Him in measure, but there are many other realms of knowing to which we will soon be introduced. You may know Him, but you will know Him and know Him and know Him some more until, at last you KNOW Him. Knowing Him is the ultimate revival, knowing Him in the glory. We begin by knowing Him as Savior. We come to know Him as the Baptizer in the Holy Ghost. Then we come to know Him as Great Physician, the Healer.

We begin to know Him as Jehovah Jireh, the Great Provider. All this is just the beginning of knowing, of knowing who He really is. There is much yet to be revealed and as we follow on to know Him, we will discover Him in one new dimension after another. The glory reveals Him. It brings forth "the revelation of Jesus Christ."

Ezekiel 1:26-28 And above the firmament that was over their heads was the likeness of a throne, as the appearance of a sapphire stone: and upon the likeness of the throne was the likeness as the appearance of a man above upon it. And I saw as the colour of amber, as the appearance of fire round about within it, from the appearance of his loins even upward, and from the appearance of his loins even downward, I saw as it were the appearance of fire, and it had brightness round about.

GLORY: EXPANDING GOD'S PRESENCE: DISCOVER HOW TO MANIFEST GOD'S GLORY

As the appearance of the bow that is in the cloud in the day of rain, so was the appearance of the brightness round about. This was the appearance of the likeness of the glory of the LORD. And when I saw it, I fell upon my face, and I heard a voice of one that spake.

Nothing about God is limited. We can know Him by seeing His hands. We can know Him by seeing His feet. He shows us what we need to see at the moment.

Revelations 5:13 And every creature which is in heaven, and on the earth, and under the earth, and such as are in the sea, and all that are in them, heard I saying, Blessing, and honour, and glory, and power, be unto him that sitteth upon the throne, and unto the Lamb for ever and ever.

When you have seen the glory of the Lord upon the throne, nothing can ever cause you to fear again. I had seen the King upon His throne; why should I be concerned for the future? If you haven't moved into that revelation yet, do it today. It doesn't take long. Once you have seen the Lord you will be compelled to allow His fire to burn in you and one of the reasons you do that is because you want to continue to see Him. You want the seeing of Him to be a continual experience.

Although, on this occasion, I only saw Him from the waist down, I instantly knew that He was totally in control that He rules over the affairs of this world and I knew that He was bringing forth revival. Revival is bringing an acceleration of the purposes of God in the Earth and an important part of that revival is the revealing to us of our Bridegroom. The revelation of Jesus Christ is a very personal thing. It's not enough for you to read what I have seen or what others have seen. You can hear someone else speak of their experiences in Heaven, but it's not enough. Unless you are seeing in the realm of the Spirit yourself, you won't be satisfied. You will only be frustrated. But you don't have to be. God is doing it so easily for all of us. You don't have to be someone special to receive this revelation. In some of the smaller congregations where people are relatively unknown, they are experiencing wonderful revelation. With some of those who are not having a revelation of the Lord, it is because they are not taking time to seek Him. They feel that they just don't have time to wait in the presence of the Lord.

But nothing could be more important than the revelation of Jesus. When you have seen Him, great truths can be made known to you, even without reading. In the anointing, say to the Lord, "Would You show me something wonderful about Yourself that I've never known before? Would you reveal some little aspect of Your character to me? Could I see Your hands close up?" Does the Lord have time to be with you? Absolutely. We know that He is great and that "the heaven of heavens cannot contain him." But we also know that He delighted to sit down by the woman at the well and commune with her heart to heart. And He will do the same for you. Begin to notice how many times in His earthly ministry Jesus took time to deal with individuals. There were crowds, but He was interested in the individuals within those crowds. There were multitudes, but He loved the individuals within those multitudes. He revealed great truths to the crowds, but He was just as concerned to reveal great truths to the individuals in those crowds. He did not deal only with the scholarly or the great.

He loved the little people, the new people, the common people. The greatest revelations of the ministry of Jesus. If you are willing to ponder the deep things of God, He is willing to stop by your well and reveal Himself to you. Say to Him, "I want to consider You, Lord."

Revelations 4:1, 2 After this I looked, and, behold, a door was opened in heaven: and the first voice which I heard was as it were of a trumpet talking with me; which said, Come up hither, and I will shew thee things which must be hereafter. And immediately I was in the spirit: and, behold, a throne was set in heaven, and one sat on the throne.

You want to know Him and you want to be ready for the Marriage of the Lamb. We want to know the intimate details about a person. We want to know the secrets of their hearts before we are willing to commit ourselves to them for life. The Lord, our heavenly Bridegroom, is willing to reveal His secrets to us through the Spirit.

This is the day of revelation. This is the day of God's glory. This is the day when God wants to make Himself known to us. When you love someone, you want to know everything you can about that person. It isn't enough just to look at them. Your heart yearns to know more and more. These are days of love for the Body of Christ. We are not only learning to know the King in His majesty, but we are also coming to know Him as Bridegroom and Lover, the Beloved of our souls. There are many things that we want to consider about God's Glory and all that we learn is to know in Revival Glory.

Don't miss out!

Visit the website below and you can sign up to receive emails whenever Bill Vincent publishes a new book. There's no charge and no obligation.

https://books2read.com/r/B-A-XHBC-TYLBB

BOOKS 2 READ

Connecting independent readers to independent writers.

Also by Bill Vincent

Building a Prototype Church: Divine Strategies Released
Experience God's Love: By Revival Waves of Glory School of the Supernatural
Glory: Expanding God's Presence
Glory: Increasing God's Presence
Glory: Kingdom Presence of God
Glory: Pursuing God's Presence
Glory: Revival Presence of God
Rapture Revelations: Jesus Is Coming
The Prototype Church: Heaven's Strategies for Today's Church
The Secret Place of God's Power
Transitioning Into a Prototype Church: New Church Arising
Spiritual Warfare Made Simple
Aligning With God's Promises
A Closer Relationship With God
Armed for Battle: Spiritual Warfare Battle Commands
Breakthrough of Spiritual Strongholds
Desperate for God's Presence: Understanding Supernatural Atmospheres
Destroying the Jezebel Spirit: How to Overcome the Spirit Before It Destroys You!
Discerning Your Call of God

Glory: Expanding God's Presence: Discover How to Manifest God's Glory

Glory: Kingdom Presence Of God: Secrets to Becoming Ambassadors of Christ

Satan's Open Doors: Access Denied

Spiritual Warfare: The Complete Collection

The War for Spiritual Battles: Identify Satan's Strategies

Understanding Heaven's Court System: Explosive Life Changing Secrets

A Godly Shaking: Don't Create Waves

Faith: A Connection of God's Power

Global Warning: Prophetic Details Revealed

Overcoming Obstacles

Spiritual Leadership: Kingdom Foundation Principles

Glory: Revival Presence of God: Discover How to Release Revival Glory

Increasing Your Prophetic Gift: Developing a Pure Prophetic Flow

Millions of Churches: Why Is the World Going to Hell?

The Supernatural Realm: Discover Heaven's Secrets

The Unsearchable Riches of Christ: Chosen to be Sons of God

Deep Hunger: God Will Change Your Appetite Toward Him

Defeating the Demonic Realm

Glory: Increasing God's Presence: Discover New Waves of God's Glory

Growing In the Prophetic: Developing a Prophetic Voice

Healing After Divorce: Grace, Mercy and Remarriage

Love is Waiting

Awakening of Miracles: Personal Testimonies of God's Healing Power

Deception and Consequences Revealed: You Shall Know the Truth and the Truth Shall Set You Free
Overcoming the Power of Lust
Are You a Follower of Christ: Discover True Salvation
Cover Up and Save Yourself: Revealing Sexy is Not Sexy
Heaven's Court System: Bringing Justice for All
The Angry Fighter's Story: Harness the Fire Within
The Wrestler: The Pursuit of a Dream
Beginning the Courts of Heaven: Understanding the Basics
Breaking Curses: Legal Rights in the Courts of Heaven
Writing and Publishing a Book: Secrets of a Christian Author
How to Write a Book: Step by Step Guide
The Anointing: Fresh Oil of God's Presence
Spiritual Leadership: Kingdom Foundation Principles Second Edition
The Courts of Heaven: How to Present Your Case
The Jezebel Spirit: Tactics of Jezebel's Control
Heaven's Angels: The Nature and Ranking of Angels
Don't Know What to Do?: Discover Promotion in the Wilderness
Word of the Lord: Prophetic Word for 2020
The Coronavirus Prophecy
Increase Your Anointing: Discover the Supernatural
Apostolic Breakthrough: Birthing God's Purposes
The Healing Power of God: Releasing the Power of the Holy Spirit
The Secret Place of God's Power: Revelations of God's Word
The Rapture: Details of the Second Coming of Christ
Increase of Revelation and Restoration: Reveal, Recover & Restore

Restoration of the Soul: The Presence of God Changes Everything
Building a Prototype Church: The Church is in a Season of Profound of Change
Keys to Receiving Your Miracle: Miracles Happen Today
The Resurrection Power of God: Great Exploits of God
Transitioning to the Prototype Church: The Church is in a Season of Profound of Transition
Waves of Revival: Expect the Unexpected
The Stronghold of Jezebel: A True Story of a Man's Journey
Glory: Pursuing God's Presence: Revealing Secrets
Like a Mighty Rushing Wind
Steps to Revival
Supernatural Power
The Goodness of God
The Secret to Spiritual Strength
The Glorious Church's Birth: Understanding God's Plan For Our Lives
God's Presence Has a Profound Impact On Us
Spiritual Battles of the Mind: When All Hell Breaks Loose, Heaven Sends Help
A Godly Shaking Coming to the Church: Churches are Being Rerouted
Relationship with God in a New Way
The Spirit of God's Anointing: Using the Holy Spirit's Power in You
The Magnificent Church: God's Power Is Being Manifested
Miracles Are Awakened: Today is a Day of Miracles
Prepared to Fight: The Battle of Deliverance
The Journey of a Faithful: Adhering to the teachings of Jesus Christ

Ascension to the Top of Spiritual Mountains: Putting an End to Pain Cycles

After Divorce Recovery: When I Think of Grace, I Think of Mercy and Remarriage

A Greater Sense of God's Presence: Learn How to Make God's Glory Visible

Do Not Allow the Enemy to Steal: To a Crown of Righteousness, a Crown of Thorns

There Are Countless Churches: What is the Cause of Global Doom?

Creating a Model Church: The Church is Undergoing Considerable Upheaval

Developing Your Prophetic Ability: Creating a Flow of Pure Prophetic Intent

Christ's Limitless Riches Are Unsearchable: God Has Chosen Us to Be His Sons

Faith is a Link Between God's Might and Ours

Increasing the Presence of God: The Revival of the End-Times Is Approaching

Getting a Prophecy for Yourself: Unlocking Your Prophecies with Prophetic Keys

Getting Rid of the Jezebel Spirit: Before the Spirit Destroys You, Here's How to Overcome It!

Getting to Know Heaven's Court System: Secrets That Will Change Your Life

God's Resurrected Presence: Revival Glory is Being Released

God's Presence In His Kingdom: Secrets to Becoming Christ's Ambassadors

God's Healing Ability: The Holy Spirit's Power is Being Released

God's Power of Resurrection: God's Great Exploits

Heaven's Supreme Court: Providing Equal Justice for All

Increasing God's Presence in Our Lives: God's Glory Has Reached New Heights

Jezebel's Stronghold: This is the Story of an Actual Man's Journey

Making the Shift to the Model Church: The Church Is In the Midst of a Major Shift

Overcoming Lust's Influence: The Way to Victory

Pursuing God's Presence: Disclosing Information

The Plan to Take Over America: Restoring, We the People and the Power of God

Revelation and Restoration Are Increasing: The Process That Reveals, Recovers, and Restores

Burn In the Presence of the Lord

Revival Tidal Waves: Be Prepared for the Unexpected

Taking down the Demonic Realm: Curses and Revelations of Demonic Spirits

The Apocalypse: Details about Christ's Second Coming

The Hidden Resource of God's Power

The Open Doors of Satan: Access is Restricted

The Secrets to Getting Your Miracle

The Truth About Deception and Its Consequences

The Universal World: Discover the Mysteries of Heaven

Warning to the World: Details of Prophecies Have Been Revealed

Wonders and Significance: God's Glory in New Waves

Word of the Lord

Why Is There No Lasting Revival: It's Time For the Next Move of God

A Double New Beginning: A Prophetic Word, the Best Is Yet to Come

Your Most Productive Season Ever: The Anointing to Get Things Done

Break Free From Prison: No More Bondage for the Saints

Breaking Strongholds: Taking Steps to Freedom

Carrying the Glory of God: Igniting the End Time Revival

Breakthrough Over the Enemies Attack on Resources: An Angel Called Breakthrough

Days of Breakthrough: Your Time is Now

Empowered For the Unprecedented: Extraordinary Days Ahead

The Ultimate Guide to Self-Publishing: How to Write, Publish, and Promote Your Book for Free

The Art of Writing: A Comprehensive Guide to Crafting Your Masterpiece

The Non-Fiction Writer's Guide: Mastering Engaging Narratives

Spiritual Leadership (Large Print Edition): Kingdom Foundation Principles

Desperate for God's Presence (Large Print Edition): Understanding Supernatural Atmospheres

From Writer to Marketer: How to Successfully Promote Your Self-Published Book

Unleashing Your Inner Author: A Step-by-Step Guide to Crafting Your Own Bestseller

Becoming a YouTube Sensation: A Guide to Success

The Art of Content Creation: Tips and Tricks for YouTube

Watch for more at
https://revivalwavesofgloryministries.com/.

About the Author

Bill Vincent is no stranger to understanding the power of God. Not only has he spent over twenty years as a Minister with a strong prophetic anointing, he is now also an Apostle and Author with Revival Waves of Glory Ministries in Litchfield, IL. Along with his wife, Tabitha, he, leads a team providing apostolic oversight in all aspects of ministry, including service, personal ministry and Godly character.

Bill offers a wide range of writings and teachings from deliverance, to experiencing presence of God and developing Apostolic cutting edge Church structure. Drawing on the power of the Holy Spirit through years of experience in Revival, Spiritual Sensitivity, and deliverance ministry, Bill now focuses mainly on pursuing the Presence of God and breaking the power of the devil off of people's lives.

His books 50 and counting has since helped many people to overcome the spirits and curses of Satan. For more information or to keep up with Bill's latest releases, please visit www.revivalwavesofgloryministries.com. To contact Bill, feel free to follow him on twitter @revivalwaves.

Read more at https://revivalwavesofgloryministries.com/.

About the Publisher

Accepting manuscripts in the most categories. We love to help people get their words available to the world.

Revival Waves of Glory focus is to provide more options to be published. We do traditional paperbacks, hardcovers, audio books and ebooks all over the world. A traditional royalty-based publisher that offers self-publishing options, Revival Waves provides a very author friendly and transparent publishing process, with President Bill Vincent involved in the full process of your book. Send us your manuscript and we will contact you as soon as possible.

Contact: Bill Vincent at rwgpublishing@yahoo.com

CPSIA information can be obtained
at www.ICGtesting.com
Printed in the USA
BVHW041130120523
664065BV00001B/143